Family Child Care Homes

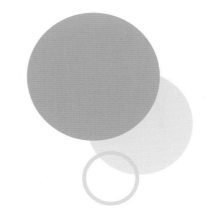

Family Child Care Homes

Creative Spaces for Children to Learn

LINDA J. ARMSTRONG

Redleaf Press®
www.redleafpress.org
800-423-8309

Published by Redleaf Press
10 Yorkton Court
St. Paul, MN 55117
www.redleafpress.org

First edition 2012
Cover design by Jim Handrigan
Cover photograph courtesy of Susan Gifford
Interior design by Erin Kirk New
Typeset in Janson Text and Scala Sans
Interior photographs by John Armstrong, except on pages ii, 6, 16, 25, 32 (left),
    37 (bottom), 49, 84, 86 (bottom), 87, 109, 153 (bottom), 156, and 166,
    by Tim Perpich
Illustrations by Janet S. Ballard except on pages 99–101, by Victoria Helbling
Printed in the United States of America
20 19 18 17 16 15 14 13   2 3 4 5 6 7 8 9

Library of Congress Cataloging-in-Publication Data
Armstrong, Linda J.
    Family child care homes : creative spaces for children to learn / Linda J.
  Armstrong. — 1st ed.
      p. cm.
    Includes bibliographical references.
    ISBN 978-1-60554-075-7 (alk. paper)
    1. Family day care—Planning. 2. Family day care—Management.   I. Title.
  HQ778.5.A755 2011
  362.71'2068—dc22
                                                                    2011004164

Printed on acid-free paper

This book is dedicated to all the family child care

providers who welcome children and families

into their homes every day. I have the greatest

respect and admiration for you and hope this

book will create interest in keeping the feeling

of home in family child care.

Contents

Preface

"Welcome home!" "Home is where the heart is." "Mi casa es su casa." All these familiar quotations convey one thought—home is where we feel a sense of safety and belonging. Our homes take on our personalities with colors and patterns that range from vibrant palettes and polka dots to muted hues and subtle stripes. We live in log cabins, manufactured houses, small townhouses, and towering apartment buildings. However, the term *home* means more than physical space; *home* is a feeling that comes over us when we think about being inside with people we love. I have coined the term *homestyle* to refer to a feeling we have when seeing or thinking about home.

Every week family child care (FCC) providers open their homes to over one million children under age five in over 238,000 family child care homes. This accounts for 9 percent of the children of working mothers (National Association of Child Care Resources and Referral Agencies 2010). Parents interviewed were pleased that their children received individual attention in a home-based setting (Layzer, Goodson, and Brown-Lyons 2007). Parents with children in family child care ranked the home environment as one of the major indicators of satisfaction of care (Morrissey and Banghart 2007).

All too often, however, the look and feel of home is ignored and family child care environments take on the appearance of mini child development centers. Out go small wooden tables, rocking chairs, and baskets of books. In come plastic stackable chairs, vinyl resting mats, oversized bookcases, and large circle-time rugs. Walls display commercial photos of children in India or Nepal, interest center signs are placed at adult eye level, and mobiles hang from ceilings everywhere. For whatever reason, many FCC environments have lost their homestyle atmosphere. It is time to bring back the feeling of home in family child care.

This book is written for those of you who operate a family child care in your own home. It challenges you to set aside center-based notions of what a child care setting should include and helps you think more deeply about the real advantages of providing child care in your family's home setting. I hope you will be inspired to make creative and exciting learning environments that capture the feeling of home for children. The book offers many practical suggestions to arrange furniture, store materials, declutter the child care space, and select items that address the needs of all children in your care. Checklists and resources for quick reference help identify problematic areas in the environment, set up multiuse learning areas, and locate additional sources of information.

The ideas and suggestions presented here are based on my visits to hundreds of FCC homes, input from FCC providers, and years of motherhood and now grandmotherhood. Well-respected research and other proven sources of sound family child care and child development practices have been incorporated and referenced throughout the book. This resource is not meant to be a decorating book for an "extreme makeover." Rather, I hope the material presented will open your eyes to the many ways you can take advantage of the intimate feeling of home as you design environments where children love to be and love to learn.

As a busy family child care provider, your time and energy is spent on the children in your care and your family. Finding time to think about, research, budget for, and make changes in your home environment may seem an impossible task, so this book does the legwork for you. You will find suggestions and ideas you can use within the context of limited time, energy, and money. Read on for creative ways to capitalize on the best aspect of the child care you provide—a homestyle family environment, a place that feels like home for both the children in your care and the families who bring them from their homes to yours.

Acknowledgments

As I have found out in the last few months, writing a book involves much more than an author putting thoughts into writing. While my name is listed as the author, many others have played significant roles in getting this project completed. For keeping me going in the right direction, I want to thank Melissa Beard, Paula Cox, Susan Gifford, Kristine LaPorte, and Carolynn Perpich, who served as my advisers and the voices of common sense. I'd also like to thank Jean Anderson, Tammy Bolin, Tamara Boulier, Melissa Beard, Susan Gifford, Brittney Jarrell, Tracie Lane, Kristine LaPorte, Carolynn Perpich, and Charity Richardson for allowing me to share photographs of their child care programs in this book. For having faith in me when I didn't have it in myself, I am very grateful to David Heath and Kyra Ostendorf at Redleaf Press. I want to thank my good friend since kindergarten, Jan Ballard, for creating such beautiful illustrations. She read my mind and created the perfect drawings for making the text so visual. A huge thank you to everyone at Community Playthings and Environments, Inc., for the loan and donation of their materials, which added much to the providers' homes and thereby to the photos in this book.

I thank my own daughters, Sarah and Beth, who have been the joy of my life; their playrooms were the first of my designs for child care learning spaces. But most of all, I want to thank my husband and best friend of forty-eight years, who has listened so patiently and reassured me constantly that I really could write this book.

Defining Your Homestyle Environment

The unique opportunity of having a homestyle child care environment takes on two forms: promoting the feeling of home and supporting the learning needs of the children. The goal is to create or recreate your family child care space as an extension of your home rather than a place of business.

Many of you reading this book already have a family child care program up and running, whereas others are just getting started. If you are a new provider, read appendix A first for information to help you and your family members start your new business venture. Those of you who have already achieved licensure, accreditation, or Child Development Associate (CDA) credentialing may find that the information in appendix A provides a good review or a new perspective on the family child care profession.

If you already have children in care, I encourage you to complete the following questionnaire to help guide your thoughts and decisions as you proceed through this book.

The environment is viewed as the third teacher, with the power to provoke curiosity and learning and encourage interaction.

—NORTH AMERICAN REGGIO EMILIA ALLIANCE

A Day in the Life of Your Program Questionnaire

ARRIVAL TIME

- What is the first thing the children and their families see or hear when they enter your home?

  _____

- Is there at least one place for each child's personal belongings?

  _____

- Is this space accessible for the child's use without adult assistance?

  _____

- Can children find and return their belongings without adult assistance?

  _____

- What behaviors do the children display when they leave their families and start their day with you?

  _____

  _____

  _____

- What areas do children go to when they arrive?

  _____

  _____

  _____

PLAYTIME

- Is the environment in your home supportive of children as independent learners?

  _____

- Are there "traffic jams" as children go from one place to another?

  _____

- Do the pathways disrupt play areas?

  _____

- Are the play areas too big or too small for the number of children in them?

  _____

- What areas are used most? Least? Not at all?

  _____

  _____

  _____

From *Family Child Care Homes: Creative Spaces for Children to Learn* by Linda J. Armstrong, © 2012.
Published by Redleaf Press, www.redleafpress.org. This page may be reproduced for provider use only.

MEALTIME/SNACKTIME

- Is the mealtime environment relaxed and enjoyable?

  _____

- Is there enough space for everyone (including you) to sit comfortably and promote conversation during meals?

  _____

- Is the room or eating space bright and attractive?

  _____

- Have you selected and arranged food in ways that make meals interesting and fun?

  _____

QUIET TIME

- Are there places for children to be alone?

  _____

- Are there places where children can be with only one or two other children?

  _____

- Can you change the mood of an area by changing the amount of light or rearranging furniture?

  _____

ACTIVITY TIME

- Is there an open area large enough for all the children to sit, dance, or play together?

  _____

- Are materials readily available and easy for the children to find and return?

  _____

OUTDOOR TIME

- Does your outdoor environment connect children with nature through natural elements?

  _____

- Are there places outdoors where children can be involved in a variety of sensory experiences such as smelling flowers, touching textural things, or hearing animal sounds?

  _____

- Does the outdoor environment support both children's quiet or passive play and their active play?

  _____

From *Family Child Care Homes: Creative Spaces for Children to Learn* by Linda J. Armstrong, © 2012.
Published by Redleaf Press, www.redleafpress.org. This page may be reproduced for provider use only.

Ten Messages a Quality Environment Conveys

For us adults, living each day sometimes takes everything we have. We would all like to get away to a place where everyone knows us and we can relax in the comfort of being supported and loved. The same is true for children. The feeling of togetherness found in FCC programs is one that no other group care setting can duplicate. You can instill those warm, secure feelings for the children in your care by creating a quality environment that encourages learning while being a place that feels like home. A quality learning environment should send these important messages to children:

1   This is a good place to be. You belong here.

2   You can trust all the big people in this place.

3   You can be independent and do many exciting things that help you learn.

4   You can get away and be by yourself or be with your friends whenever you want to.

5   There is a place where you can be away from younger children or be alone with just your brother or sister.

6   This is a safe place to explore and try out your ideas.

7   Everything here is for you and you can use whatever you like.

8   You know where things are and they're always in the same place.

9   This is a happy place that helps you learn new things.

10   Somebody knows you and knows what you like to do.

Environment Defined

We hear a lot about environments in family child care, but have you ever stopped to ask exactly what the term *environment* means? You may be surprised by the answer. Experts in early childhood education write that the environment is everything the child touches, uses, and experiences every day (Isbell and Exelby 2001; Curtis and Carter 2003; Greenman 2005). Without a doubt, a home setting is the most familiar and long-remembered learning environment a child will have.

If we all stop to think about our early learning years, we will remember the rich and perhaps even the painful learning we experienced at home.

The feeling of togetherness found in FCC
programs is one that no other group care
setting can duplicate.

I crawled into the laundry chute one day and learned how to problem solve very quickly. Then there was the day a beautiful bug on my mother's tomato plants became my newest pet and, a few days later, I found out it was the cause of small warts all over my hands. I also learned to make paste out of flour and water and a spacious playhouse out of a refrigerator box.

Young children learn about the principles of water from playing in the bathtub. They learn about size relationships from stacking the pots and pans from the kitchen cabinet. Art techniques are learned from spreading applesauce and pudding all over the dining room table. Over the years, the dining room table will also be a laboratory table for science fair experiments and tons of homework. The laws of physics are investigated and discoveries about plants and animals are made in the backyard. This type of experiential learning is natural and meaningful to children without the need for expensive commercial learning materials.

Whether inside or outside, a safe and exciting environment encourages children to wander and wonder.

Over the past ten years, in an attempt to meet educational and environmental standards and regulations, family child care environments have lost their homestyle atmosphere. It is time to bring back the feeling of home in family child care. Homestyle environments are intimate and enriching, stimulating and cozy. They encourage children to be involved within the space, with each other, and with materials. Whether you have one room or many rooms for your child care program, making the most of each space is important. Your home should say to each child, "I'm glad you're here today."

A welcoming feeling starts at this provider's front door.

These child care spaces are shared with the providers' families.

These child care spaces have been created just for FCC programs; the spaces are not in areas of the home shared by family members.

This soft, comfortable place invites a child to
slow down for a while.

The feeling of home comes through with furniture made of wood and natural fibers on this porch space.

This bathroom invites children with
a feeling of whimsy and fun.

Warning Signs of Inappropriate Environments

Warning signs indicate that something about the environment is inappropriate for children. An environment is not working for children if they do the following:

- consistently run in the child care space
- wander around looking for something to do
- repeat the same activity over and over
- remain uninvolved and unable to stick with an activity
- fight over toys and materials
- use materials destructively or inappropriately
- shout from one area to another
- crawl under tables or on furniture
- resist cleaning up
- constantly depend on adults to supply the things they need

Other warning signs indicating the environment needs a change include the following:

- The same materials are out day after day and the children appear to be bored with them.
- There are no soft areas where children can get away and be by themselves.
- Materials are not attractively displayed or organized.
- Walls are cluttered with nonpurposeful displays, materials are placed above the children's eye level, or displays do not include the children's work.

○ ○ ○

As they grow, the children in your care will have many years of learning in settings away from home, including schools, churches or synagogues, ballet studios, or ball fields. Typically, these places are formally named or have an institutional feeling about them. Young children are anything but formal. They love to be down on the floor, playing under tables, or dancing in the kitchen. Early learning environments should be exciting and informal learning places, not "pre-institutions" (Shepherd and Eaton 1997). Think of your FCC environment as not just a physical space but also a place where children are encouraged to wander and to wonder. An exciting homestyle environment is one of the most important, if not *the* most important, elements that supports children's learning.

Chapter 2 presents specific elements that will help you create an environment that allows children to experience both learning and fun at the same time. Walls and halls, color and lighting, and patterns and textures are all discussed, as each is an important element in children's lives.

Activities and Questions

Go into your child care space physically (if your environment is already set up) or mentally (if you are designing the environment). What does it feel like to be a child in this place? To answer this you may need to get down on your hands and knees, or on your stomach, or sit in a low chair. Use these questions to guide you as you look at the characteristics of your environment as a child would:

1   Is the environment welcoming? Do children come through the door eagerly? What elements can you add to the environment to put out the welcome mat for children and families?

2   Have you promoted or reduced the natural hominess of your child care setting? What can you add or remove to promote a homestyle learning environment?

3   Where are the soft or cozy elements to support quiet and relaxing play?

4   Does this environment make learning fun? Are children eager to use the materials to support their learning?

5   Are all elements in the environment purposeful or are they just cute or entertaining?

6   Is this an exciting but safe place where all accessible materials tell the child "touch me, use me, and learn from me"? What items need to be added or removed?

7   Think about who shares the child care space. Is your business crowding out your family? How can you keep the balance between a home-based business and a family-centered home?

Designing Environments for Learning and Fun

As adults, we are able to verbalize how we feel in a certain place. Young children, who are still learning how to verbalize their feelings, express feelings through their behavior. Watch children as they come into a kitchen where cookies or cabbage has just been prepared and you'll easily see how the environment supports their feelings about a place. The environment is everything we see, touch, smell, hear, and interact with. It's human nature to want to stay in places that make us feel happy or welcome and to leave places that make us feel uncomfortable or unwelcome. This chapter focuses on the mood or atmosphere of your child care space.

Anita Rui Olds (2001, 289), a pioneer in innovative environmental design for children, expressed the importance of setting the mood for children in the following way: "Aim to match the mood of each area to the physical energy children expend in performing its activity. For example, tranquil activities occur best in warm, soft, textured spaces; expansive activities require spaces that are cooler, harder, and more vibrant in tone. The

The spirit of a place depends more on the presence of natural light than perhaps any other factor.

—ANITA RUI OLDS

ultimate goal is a room with multiple activity areas, each of which has a unique spirit of place. Then, as children go from place to place within the room's four walls, they can experience spaces that are soft and hard, dark and light, cold and warm, colorful and bland, large and small, noisy and quiet."

The open doors allow children to move freely from one room to another. They also allow the provider to maintain supervision from nearly any vantage point.

Some spaces scream out to children "Run!" while others whisper "Sit a while." Albert Mehrabian (1976) developed the concept of *environmental load* as a way to understand why adults and children react in predictable ways in certain locations. *High-load* places are subways, amusement parks, parades, and gymnasiums, which trigger excitement, confusion, and rapid heart rates. *Low-load* places such as churches, libraries, and bedrooms are just the opposite. They encourage relaxation, calmness, and slow respiration.

Use the information in this chapter to help you think about the environmental load in your child care space. How do the color, lighting, textures, and patterns load the environment for learning and fun?

Walls and Halls

When I visit child care spaces in homes, schools, centers, or commercial buildings, I am amazed at what is on the walls. Typically, the wall displays are neither meaningful to nor supportive of the children's learning. Required postings such as fire and safety information don't have to be the first thing you see. Even displays of children's work or photographs that children connect with are often arranged so they end up as visual clutter. For wall displays to be effective and functional in the learning environment, they must be more than color that fills the surface. Go into your child care space and look at the walls. What do you see? You might see the following:

- commercial photos of people the children don't know
- learning posters that include shapes, numbers, letters, and so on
- cartoon or theme park characters
- children's artwork or examples of their prewriting or writing

Many providers use learning posters, commercial photos, or interest center signs in their child care space. Some wall displays are cute—cartoon or theme park characters or seasonal posters. Some displays include photos of people the children don't know dressed in exotic clothing, riding elephants, or eating strange foods, meant to tell them about foreign cultures. The calendar might spell out the day of the week for pre-toddlers who can't read, and the seasons chart may tell them it's spring even though there are still snowdrifts outside. Some displays are only words that tell everyone where the block center or the library is located even though the children cannot read them and adults don't need them. Such displays are often neither helpful nor useful to the children.

Some displays are definitely needed, however; one example is a picture-word combination of labeling that helps children locate and return their playthings to the right place. Interestingly enough, I have yet to find a regulation or standard stipulating that interest-center signage is required. One accrediting agency indicated that these signs could encourage prewriting skills in preschoolers but they were not a requirement.

In my experience, most wall displays in family child care settings have been put up to project a child development center appearance (or perhaps to hide holes in the walls). Many providers feel families expect the child care space to have such displays. But no matter how you look at it, the families you serve have chosen your program because it is in a *home* and not in a commercial building. A homestyle feeling can begin with the four walls of your child care space.

These two photos are from a provider who wants to change her child care space to make it more homelike and age appropriate for the children in her care.

This small magnetic board is made from two sheets of galvanized steel and attached to the wall.

A mural, used to compare children's growth and height, softens a long wall. Note that it is on the lower part of the wall at the children's eye level.

These drawings show off children's creativity and liven up a wall.

Take down all displays that have no meaning or interest for the children. Your child care space is not a place for cute, commercial, or craft store wall hangings. Limiting the number and location of displays can open up the entire room. Use your walls and hallways to display the children's creative talents and writing activities (especially important for school-age children). Take and display photographs of the children at work and play during the day. Documentation of what the children have done, their interests, and their families must be displayed respectfully and at a level where the children can enjoy and, yes, even touch it.

Here are some quick tips to help you with designing your walls and halls:

- For fire safety reasons, leave 60–80 percent of your walls free of any hanging items.

- Put all regulations, guidelines, certificates, and business policies that don't require posting into a photo album or attractive binder in your welcoming area for visitors and families to read.

- If the children are old enough, ask them what they would like to put on the walls. This lets you know what each child feels is important.

- Cluster children's work together in plastic frames with removable backing to create an Artists in Residence Gallery. To showcase the artists, include photos with the framed work.

- Keep current information on your hall bulletin board to prevent it from becoming a bulletin *bored*.

Portions of this wall are left blank to reduce fire risk.

These framed certificates are ready to be read by all families and visitors.

Children will feel proud when they see their artwork hanging in galleries like these.

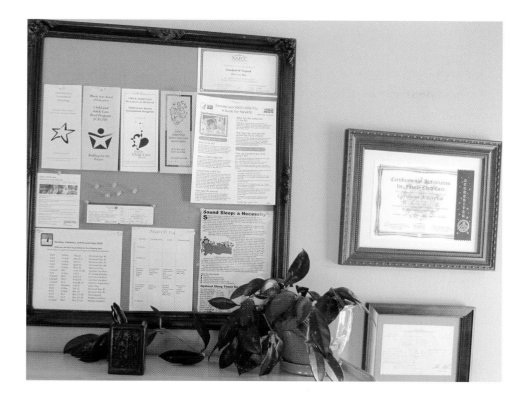

An updated bulletin board keeps parents involved and interested in your child care.

Ask yourself the following questions about what you see on the walls in your child care space:

- At what eye level are these displays located?

- How many of them have been up for more than a month? Two months? Even longer?

- Are they faded or torn?

- How many of the displays relate to your business practice, for example, your certificate to operate, menus, policies, or standards?

- How many photos do you have of the children in your care? Do they show the children in child care activities, with their families, with you?

- How often do you see the children and their families looking at any of the displays on your walls? Have they been up so long they've become wallpaper?

Always ask yourself, "Why display these on the wall? Is there a purpose or need for them?" Be critical, choose carefully, and change wall displays often to keep the children interested. Your child care space is all about children—even the walls—so put displays where they can admire them, learn from them, and even touch them.

Color

Color creates a rainbow of life. Our world would be bleak and drab if we saw everything only in black and white. Color gives character and feeling to surroundings. Phrases such as feeling "in the pink" or being "red with rage" or "green with envy" tell us something about a color's characteristic effect. Most of us have a favorite color that brings back memories or creates a certain mood in us. Color can drastically change how we feel about where we are.

Think of a box of crayons that has many different tones of the same color. There are high-tone and low-tone colors. Typically, high-tone colors, sometimes called dramatic colors, are bold, pure, bright, and vibrant. High-tone colors are often found in fast food restaurants, on the outside of stores, and in other places with high activity levels. High tones or high-intensity colors are also known as *pure* colors because they have no other colors mixed with them—specifically white or black. They are usually the colors of the color wheel: red, orange, yellow, green, blue, and purple.

On the other hand, low-tone colors, often referred to as pastels or muted colors, are found in libraries, churches, and babies' rooms. Places with low-tone colors convey a feeling of softness and quiet. Warm tones (colors) are those that suggest things in life we know to be warm, such as red and orange being the colors of fire or yellow representing the sun. Places with warmer colors such as red, orange, and yellow excite children. Indoor children's playgrounds and fun houses are perfect examples of the physiological change children experience when they're in places with dramatic, high-tone colors. Cool tones are those associated with being cold in life, such as ice cubes taking on a bluish color or green grass always being cool, or your lips turning bluish-purple when you're really cold.

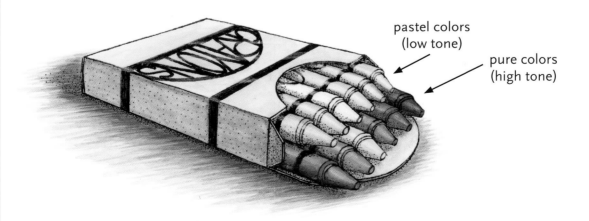

pastel colors
(low tone)

pure colors
(high tone)

The soft, warm wall color of this room gives it a relaxed, homey feel.

Most children love bright or pure-tone colors until they're about age ten (Gilberg 2000). While it's true that children need visual stimuli, these color tones can make children hyperactive and exhausted or cause them to shut down their senses against the intensity of the color. Vivid colors make it difficult for children to focus or concentrate on one thing for long. Studies have found that blind children sense color and show behavior changes depending on the color of a room; it is thought this happens through a perceived difference and warmth coming from the surface of walls or objects that are colored (Daggett, Cobble, and Gertel 2008).

Children react to color in ways that affect their behavior and learning, so we must look carefully at both the color and tone (hue) of colors used in child care settings. Think of the existing colors you have in your child care space, including both the walls and the floors. Are they high-tone or low-tone colors? Because children react physiologically to color, it can create moods and define activity levels. Cool colors, such as pale green or blue, have a very calming effect. Warm colors such as red and yellow stimulate activity. Considered colorless and neutral, gray has very limited color-mood associations. It is a restful color that fades into the background of the environment and is the perfect color for walls. Results of research have indicated

The carefully chosen wall, floor, and furniture colors in this well-designed environment support children's learning.

that bubblegum pink is another calming color. It was found to subdue violent prisoners in seconds by reducing their muscle strength and calming their behavior (Olds 2001).

Color can be used to define spaces by tying places together, creating boundaries, or defining territory. This coding function can help children find activity areas or return toys, games, and books to the appropriate places. For example, yellow might define the circle-time area, whereas orange defines the area for meals and snacks. Keep in mind, however, that using too many colors to define activity spaces can create an overwhelming kaleidoscope of colors that actually does more harm than good. Color should be kept in balance and used purposefully to support children's learning and well-being.

Using white or light beige opens up a small space. Bright or intense warm colors pull in walls and create a cozier feeling. If you choose to use bright colors, limit them to small areas or alcoves. Bright or intense colors stimulate and excite most people, including young children (Greenman 2005; Olds 2001). Walls that are neutral and light are recommended for child care spaces. Off-white, beige, or light gray walls set the background for displays of children's work, which is typically done with bright, vivid colors.

Warm colors convey a happy mood and direct children's attention, whereas cool colors help children rest and relax. Here are some examples of the psychological effect color can have on young children:

- Bright red has been found to create excitement and even promote aggression.

- Orange stimulates appetite and restores energy.

- Yellow is a happy color and promotes conversation and overall well-being.

- Green is the most restful color for the eye and has a calming effect on children.

- Blue is cold and even depressing when used in large areas, but it is soothing and calming when used as an accent color.

- Red-violet (purple) spaces create energy in children, but blue-violet spaces should be avoided, as that color depletes children's energy.

- White softened with small amounts of cream or light gray creates a natural, muted, or gentle tone that is restful for children's eyes.

- Brown aids children's concentration.

COLOR WHEEL

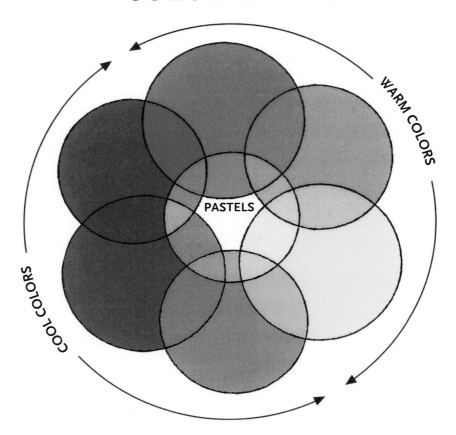

Primary colors = three basic colors from which all other colors are mixed (red, yellow, blue).

Secondary colors = colors made by mixing two primary colors together in equal amounts (green, orange, purple).

Tertiary colors = colors made when a primary and a secondary color are mixed together (such as yellow + green = yellow green).

Warm colors = red, orange, and (most) yellows.

Cool colors = blue, green, and purple.

Note: Warm colors convey a happy mood and direct children's attention, whereas cool colors help children rest and relax.

Changing your child care color scheme is one of the easiest and least expensive ways to transform the environment. Color choices for the rest of your home can be based on what pleases you and your family, but personal preferences need to be set aside when selecting colors for your child care space. Consider how colors affect children's activity levels and support their learning. In our homes, we tend to select colors that are personal favorites. Bedrooms are private places where color has a strong emotional connection and affects us accordingly. Likewise, colors support children's ability to think, create, and learn. Selecting color must be a critical component in the design of learning environments (Daggett, Cobble, and Gertel 2008).

Children are often more likely to be affected by bold colors rather than warm muted tones. Although children usually like bright colors, especially red and yellow, their preference for bright colors should not be a guiding factor when you choose your color scheme. Use bright red in small amounts as an accent color. Avoid using it in areas where the children are to rest or need to focus their attention. Orange is good for circle time and eating areas. Green is a good color for rest and quiet areas. Creamy whites are best for walls and ceilings. Brown is a great color for flooring because it is neutral and will complement other colors used on walls or as accents, but its use need not be limited just to flooring.

I once taught at a school that was offered new but leftover carpeting. We were all excited until it was installed and we discovered the remnants came from the new movie theater! Because so many activities in early childhood programs take place on the floor, the bold design and patterns made us all dizzy.

Color (usually bright and pure-tone colors) can be accented in a number of inexpensive ways, such as the following:

- quilts hung on the wall
- displays of children's artwork matted on brightly colored paper
- small clear plastic bottles filled with colored water and glitter, fuzzy pom-poms, or sand
- bulletin board backing
- pillows
- area rugs
- plants and cut flowers

Colorful accents on walls and floors add brightness and interest to these child care spaces.

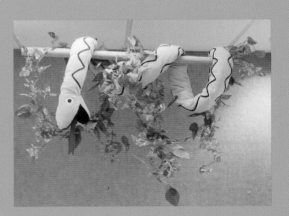

Plants are a great way to brighten up your space and bring nature indoors.

You can also paint small walls or alcoves with bright color, but don't paint window or door frames. Using bright colors on windows and door frames outlines them and draws the eye to them, which can result in the children giving the windows and doors too much attention and focus.

Now that you are a color expert, it's time to make some color choices. Before going to the paint store, write down some words that describe the mood you want to have in your child care space (for instance, you may write *nurturing* or *quiet* for your infants or *focused* or *cheery* for toddlers). Refer back to the list of the effects of color on children and choose two accent colors that support the mood you want in a particular child care space, remembering that a light, neutral color is a must for your walls. Paint is definitely

This small, bright alcove offers children an inviting place to read and relax.

the quickest, least expensive way to change an environment. When choosing the finish of paint, note these features:

- Matte finishes tend to absorb light and make the room more saturated with color.

- Glossy finishes reflect light and are more durable and washable.

- Chalkboard paint applied in many layers to walls, a tabletop, the back of a bookcase, or small pieces of wood allows for children's creative designs and writing skills and washes easily. Chalkboard paint can also be magnetic if metal dust is included in the paint.

Look at the colors in your child care space:

- Are the colors bright and bold or subtle and subdued?

- Is the space visually chaotic?

- What overall feeling do you get when you walk into this space?

When you are ready to choose a color, visit a paint store or a paint department in a hardware store that has a variety of wall color cards. Take home a selection of cards that you feel may work. Tape them up on the wall you are going to paint and leave them there for a week or so to see how the light, furniture, and the rest of the house are affected by the colors you've chosen. Some stores sell small containers of paint that allow you to paint a small section of a wall. Testing color this way can be important, as the color on a small card in a paint store may look dramatically different when placed on walls and ceilings in your home.

Use low-tone colors as the basic or main color palette for walls, furniture, and flooring. Then introduce more color through accents. This makes it simple to test color schemes and easier to make changes. Choosing a color scheme doesn't need to be difficult. Depending on how bright or light they are, many colors are appropriate for child care.

Balance is key in choosing colors and designing environments. For inspiration, look to nature and the many different colors and tones of the outdoors. Just as the colors of our natural world are peaceful and harmonious, you can choose colors that blend well together and are an extension of the rest of your home. In nature, no one color dominates another; the effect of light on the colors is the determining factor. Understanding how lighting and colors impact the emotions and moods of the children in your care is important.

Lighting

Light and color are inseparable. A rainbow is formed when light passes through water droplets. A prism distributes color only when light passes through it. When the amount and source of light change, colors change dramatically. When the color of lighting changes, colors are modified. Like color, lighting is extremely important. It can affect children's sense of security and comfort when they are away from their homes (Schreiber 1996).

There are two basic sources of light to consider in your child care space: natural and artificial. Natural light comes from the sun and sometimes even the moon. Sunlight has a positive effect on the health of both children and

This infant and caregiver are enjoying the benefits of natural sunlight.

adults. We simply feel better when we have sunlight. Artificial light, which comes from lightbulbs, is a supplement—not a replacement—for natural light and should be used flexibly depending on the children's activities.

Children particularly are affected by light in many ways. Children who lack prolonged or seasonal exposure to daylight can develop seasonal affective disorder (SAD) and exhibit fatigue and irritability. They might blame their behavior on external factors by saying things like someone is "picking on me." The main treatment for SAD is bright light therapy, but symptoms return when the lights are withdrawn (Mayo Clinic 2009). One study (Hathaway et al. 1992) found that children had higher achievement levels with full-spectrum lighting, which is the type of artificial light closest in wavelength to sunshine. Given all these factors related to the general well-being of children, it is extremely important that you consider the source and type of lighting in your child care space.

The type and intensity of lighting needed depends on the intended activity for the children. Daylight encourages active play, whereas softer light encourages quiet play, quiet conversations, and naps. Children should be in spaces with natural light (windows without coverings) if they are in a location on a regular basis. In general, use full-spectrum or fluorescent bulbs to create a warmer or more natural look indoors. Criteria for selecting artificial or electric light depend greatly on the purpose of the space. In areas where there is limited natural light, higher wattage light is needed to avoid eye strain when the children are reading, using manipulatives, or working on projects. Filtered or less intense light is more appropriate in areas where children are less active.

When you change the color and type of lighting, you'll find that the color of walls, toys, and furniture changes too. The whiter the light, the purer the colors. Using the proper wattage lightbulbs appropriate for specific tasks or activities in each location protects the children's eyes. Lights or lightbulbs that create a glare or shadows make it difficult for children to concentrate and are hard on their eyes. The quality and intensity of the light depend on the type and wattage of the bulbs or tubes you use. Incandescent light is what most home light fixtures use. These bulbs, which become hot and are the least energy-efficient light source, are also the closest to natural light. Compact fluorescent bulbs (CFLs) do not become hot, are the most energy efficient, and last longer than incandescent lightbulbs. The newer CFLs create a soft white light similar to that of incandescent lightbulbs. These bulbs can be used in nearly all light fixtures designed

Areas with natural light can ease eye strain and help children feel happier.

for incandescent lightbulbs. NOTE: All fluorescent lightbulbs contain mercury, which is a poisonous metal that must be disposed of at designated recycling centers. Should one break, mercury vapor that exceeds federal guidelines for exposure to mercury will be released from the bulb.

Halogen lights are being used more and more in homes because they last longer and are more energy efficient. Because of safety issues, however, I recommend that you do not use halogen lighting in any place where children can get to it. Halogen bulbs become extremely hot and, if touched, the oil from fingers can cause a bulb to explode. Safety is the number one factor to consider when choosing lighting for your child care space.

A single overhead light is usually the main source of lighting and provides enough illumination for play and fine-motor activities. If your budget allows, install track lighting that directs light to the places where it's most needed. Track lighting or recessed lighting also allows you to create indirect light, which is softer, in areas where the children are involved in quiet activities.

This recessed light, besides being attractive, helps keep quiet areas peaceful.

A secured table lamp provides light in areas away from natural light. Such a lamp is safe to use in spaces where children actively play.

Table lamps offer the warmest feeling of all types of lighting and can be used in your child care space as long as all the parts of the lamp (excluding the lightbulb, of course) are of a nonbreakable material. Plastic lamps are the best and most widely used for children. The bottom of the table lamp should be weighted so it doesn't tip over easily. If possible, secure the lamp base to the furniture (using screws or industrial-strength Velcro) to ensure stability and reduce the danger of the lamp falling on a child. As with all electrical cords, lamp cords must be completely out of the reach of children, which means you'll need to place lamps on immovable furniture pieces so cords stay safely tucked away and out of sight.

Fluorescent lights like the one pictured here can tire eyes quickly and may cause health problems.

Fluorescent lights tend to create glare by reflecting the sheen of items in the room, such as brightly colored plastic toys and furniture. Reflecting light can contribute to a more active, even frenzied mood in child care settings; light reflections can also lead to eyestrain, nervousness (especially in children with special needs), or stress in children and adults alike. Evidence suggests that flashes coming from fluorescent lights can be a source of hyperactivity in children and seizures for individuals who are seizure-prone (Erba 2006; Painter 1976). Fortunately, few homes have banks of fluorescent lighting, which are often found in buildings such as child development centers.

If you have fluorescent lights in your child care space, choose bulbs or tubes that provide a color mix that is most similar to daylight (available at lighting and hardware stores). Install covers over fixtures to lessen the harsh glare—especially in infant spaces, because the brains of infants are extremely active. Like muted color tones, soft ambient lighting will help keep babies calm. Also, consider installing dimmer switches to lower or soften the intensity of light during quiet play or rest time.

Warm-tone fluorescent tubes and draped fabric can soften lighting.

Although you may not be able to add windows or skylights to your child care space, you can maximize natural light by pulling back curtains and pulling up blinds or window shades and letting the sun shine in! All children need to see out windows and enjoy the outside world from inside. Consider putting furniture, ramps, window seats, or a short step stool in front of a window so even the youngest child can peek outdoors. Should you decide to have window seating or viewing for children, ensure the children's safety with tempered window glass or cover the glass with safety film.

Uncovered windows allow natural light to flood the child care space.

Take a few minutes to assess the lighting in your child care space and consider the following questions:

- Does a majority of light come from a ceiling light fixture?

- Are your windows covered with blinds, curtains, window shades, or anything else that prevents sunlight from streaming into the room?

- Look at the room(s) at different times of the day. Is there a glare or reflection from furniture or floors that might distract the children? To determine this, get down on your knees to see what the children see.

- Are the children typically wound up all day, do they have difficulty separating from their families, or do they complain of headaches? All of these problems may indicate high-intensity lighting issues.

If you answered "yes" to any of these questions, it's time to consider changing light sources. Here are some inexpensive ways to adjust lighting to improve children's learning and overall well-being:

- If you have fluorescent tubes, replace the white tubes with warm-tone tubes to create a softer, more welcoming feeling in the room.

- Change clear lightbulbs to lower wattage frosted ones. Due to safety hazards, halogen bulbs are NOT recommended for use in child care spaces.

- For more directed area light, replace ceiling fixtures with track lighting (use bulbs of different wattages to change the intensity of the light from each track fixture).

- When you need to repaint the ceiling, use a warm, neutral color rather than a stark white. This helps to soften the light and makes the ceiling height appear lower; these in turn make the room feel warmer and cozier.

Patterns

A few years ago I visited a provider's home, and upon entering her child care space I immediately felt light-headed and the need to put on sunglasses. After being there for a short time, I realized why: there were brightly colored curtains with teddy bears and balloons on all windows; multi-colored floor tiles; red, blue, and yellow rugs with large shapes and animals; big floor pillows with polka dots and stripes; and many colorful posters on the walls. I was feeling visual stress—the riot of colors, textures, and lighting was more than my eyes could absorb. When the children arrived, their behavior changed from calm and controlled to frenzied and erratic. It was apparent that all the patterns with their vivid contrasts created a high-intensity environmental load that was both overstimulating and distracting.

How can you use patterns and textures to best effect? The child care environment should be balanced and support children's learning; it should not be a kaleidoscopic collage that is visually chaotic and competes for the children's attention. Mehrabian's (1976) concept of environmental load explains how the amount, complexity, and intensity of environmental stimuli affect children's behavior and feelings. Obviously the environment described above had a high-load atmosphere that generated stimulation in many ways. The patterns and vivid contrasts of the colors made it difficult for both adults and children to concentrate.

Stark contrasts in colors and patterns are stimulating and are often used on infants' toys and play mats—in small amounts. When large objects or areas of a room have stark contrasts and patterns, there is too much stimulation for children and for adults. Many learning rugs that feature games, shapes, numbers, or letters are too colorful and can lead to visual overload, especially for young children from birth to age eight (Olds 2001). Very rarely have I seen a learning rug used as a tool to help children learn. Typically, the rugs are placed in interest centers for no intentional purpose.

Take a few minutes to understand the effect of patterns in your child care space by answering these questions:

* How many patterns are on curtains, rugs, and pillows?

* How many large patterns (over an inch in diameter) do you find?

* How many different patterns (such as polka dots, stripes, or checks) do you see?

* How many different colors are in the patterns?

* How many objects in the room have patterns? Look at curtains, rugs, pillows, and furniture, as well as floors and carpets.

If you answered "more than two" to any of these questions and the patterns are bright and bold, your child care space creates visual overload for children. Here are some suggestions for creating a calmer, lower-load atmosphere:

* Remove all curtains to showcase the view and bring the outdoors inside.

* Choose area or "spot" rugs that have variations of the same color (for example, tone on tone) or are harmonious with other colors in your child care space. Put them only in places where they are needed, for example, where children sit on the floor for activities.

* Cover all pillows in a pastel or neutral color to create a soft, calm feeling.

* Keep only those wall displays that offer meaning or interest to the children, for example, their artwork or photos of the children and their families. You may be surprised to find that many wall displays are not important to the children and, once taken down, make the space appear much larger and more organized.

Overstimulating and visually chaotic environments can hinder children's concentration and learning.

Individual rugs placed on the floor create a comfy and well-defined place for children to sit during group time.

The six-part pattern in this rug is ideal for defining where children sit during story time.

Texture

Did you know that your skin is the largest organ in your body and is a vital source of stimulation? The sense of touch is important in our lives from birth to death. Including tactile materials in the environment and maintaining human contact help us create a bond with each other and our surroundings. Babies love the feeling of their blankets; toddlers finger everything from their oatmeal to mud. Researchers suggest that touch is the most critical sense for children under the age of three, yet it is the one most overlooked in planning for child care settings (Olds 1997). From cool tiled floors to soft area rugs, textures that are child friendly (comfortable on their skin and bodies) add another dimension to your child care space.

Elements made of various textures that were once thought of as only adding to the aesthetics of child care settings are now considered essential in family child care spaces. Textures support the overall development of children through their sense of touch and exploration (National Association for Family Child Care 2005; Harms, Cryer, and Clifford 2007). For example, at room temperature, wood is warm and soft to the touch, whereas plastic feels cool and hard. Children's furniture manufacturers are making more products from wood and fewer from plastics. Baskets and bins made of sturdy wicker, twigs, or bamboo are being made by manufacturers of children's furniture and storage units.

Take a few minutes to texture test your indoor and outdoor child care space. Materials made from natural fibers, especially wicker and wood, must be inspected on a regular basis. Run your hand over all surfaces to check for sharp edges or deteriorating materials and remove any you feel might be potentially hazardous or harmful for children. Remember to clean and sanitize items made of natural fibers just as you do for all other materials children use. Consider the following questions:

- What covering is on your floors—wood, tile, carpet, or a combination of these?
- What types of ground cover are in the outdoor play space—grass, wood chips, asphalt, sand, concrete, or a combination of these?
- Are children able to feel a variety of materials on furniture or flooring, such as woven fabrics, wicker, wood, or plastic?
- How many different objects might the children touch during the course of a day? Do they have access to materials with textures that are soft, hard, smooth, rough, polished, and bumpy both inside and outdoors?
- Are most of the items children use or feel made from plastic?

Hopefully your answers indicate that your child care space contains a variety of textured materials that provide rich sensory experiences for the children. Materials that are responsive to touch encourage children to feel and hold them, run their fingers and toes over them, and use them. Here are some suggestions for adding even more textured materials to your child care environment:

- Wicker baskets allow children to carry manipulatives, puppets, books, or any of their learning treasures or to store materials for their use.

- Pillows can provide various fabric textures. NOTE: Pillows are not age-appropriate for children under twelve months old and should be kept out of their reach.

- Fabric books are easy to make and especially wonderful for infants. To make them, iron a variety of textured fabrics onto a heat-sensitive material and sew the pieces together down one side like a book.

- Area rugs provide different textures, such as clipped, looped, Berber, or braided materials.

- Furniture and play items can have tactilely diverse surfaces, such as plastic, wood, leather, rubber, or cloth.

- Natural items such as pebbles, plants, seeds, driftwood, seashells, and pinecones offer a rich source of textures. Be aware of small items (smaller than a Ping-Pong ball) that can cause choking for children under three years of age.

- Two or more different types of ground cover can be offered in the outdoor play area. For example, both grass and rubber mulch documented to be free of heavy metals are great for softening falls and feel good on children's knees and hands.

Open wicker baskets help children find and return a collection of small objects.

Pillows with interesting fabric add color and
make any space more comfortable.

Pieces from
nature let children
experience the
world's different
textures.

○ ○ ○

This chapter has examined how the environment and children's senses affect the way they learn. Children find numerous, nonmeaningful wall displays and stark contrasting patterns visually distracting; these may detract from successful learning experiences. Careful choice of color and light as well as textures and patterns is key to maintaining the feeling of a homestyle setting that is peaceful for both you and the children.

Chapter 3 helps you maintain the feeling of calm and order in your homestyle environment through a quick primer on organizing, storing, and rotating the materials you have available for the children.

Activities and Questions

Use the questions and suggestions below to help plan the changes you'll make to create a warm and inviting homestyle family child care environment.

1   What feeling do you get every time you go into your child care space? Is this a feeling you want to keep or change?

2   How much of the walls can be seen? What is displayed on your walls? Which displays do children look at (so are worth keeping)?

3   Pick three colors you really like—one bright (or vivid) color and two muted or softer ones to use in your child care space.

4   Do your light sources (such as windows or ceiling lights) give a cozy feel or institutional look to the area? How can you change or add simple things like small lamps to ensure adequate lighting for all tasks?

5   What patterns and textures are in the child care areas? Do these distract or support children's learning?

6   What changes would you like to make to your child care spaces? List all that come to mind.

These children and their provider are enjoying a book in a snug and relaxing place.

Organizing, Storing, and Rotating Materials

Has this ever happened to you? You want to add another prop to your dramatic play area but can't find a place for it, so you put it anywhere you can find room. Next a new hat arrives, then a puppet, a book, and a set of blocks and before you know it, you've got cluttered centers where children have to dig through materials to use them. Cleanup time becomes a battle. There's way too much "stuff" to put away in any kind of an organized system. The clutterbug has attacked your child care space and there's no longer any order, organization, or open areas. It's overwhelming and frustrating for both you and the children.

The program order should be functional, working to make life easier, better, and more productive . . . and contribute to a sense of aesthetic harmony.

—JIM GREENMAN

These cluttered areas are unattractive and unsafe for children.

The Problem with Clutter

Have you ever watched children after they have dumped all the blocks off the shelves, poured bins of toy counters on the floor, or cleared out the toy refrigerator? They're overwhelmed by what they've just done and often-times remain motionless just looking at the mess. Clutter causes anxiety, indecision, and even fear (you never know what's hidden at the bottom of the pile of dress-up clothes). In extreme cases, obvious health and safety issues exist in disorderly, unorganized child care spaces. Large amounts of clutter simply can't be cleaned around, so dust balls, mildew, and even mold grow. Food crumbs draw outside insects inside. Fire and safety hazards stem from too many wall or ceiling displays, playthings not stored on shelves or in containers, and residue on floors.

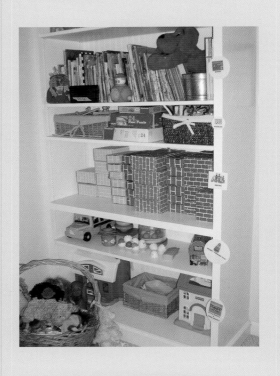

These organized, predictable environments help children feel a sense of security and independence.

Feng shui is an ancient Chinese system of aesthetics believed to help one improve life by receiving positive *chi* or energy flow. The ancient Chinese people emphasized education, thus many feng shui principles encourage and promote lifelong learning in children. According to these principles, the clutter that drains positive energy also has a variety of negative effects on children's behavior and even their health. Jim Greenman is considered one of the foremost authorities in the world on children's environments and has been involved in facility and program design for more than a hundred early childhood projects in the United States and the United Kingdom. His design recommendations are in line with feng shui principles. He believes that children's spaces need order and structure to help them make sense of the world and to allow them more experiences every day (Greenman 2006).

Bringing order and organization to your child care program entails more than just being neat or tidy. Clutter leads to a lack of energy and a lot of confusion. All areas need to be regularly purged and kept clutter free. When you clear away clutter, you create space for new materials—and the children's behavior and creativity will increase as well.

What Anita Rui Olds (1998) calls "the spirit of the place" includes selection, presentation, and maintenance of materials. The idea is to organize clutter so areas look neat, yet children know where to find things. An organized, predictable environment helps children feel a sense of security and independence. In other words, they can make sense of what's around them. Even the youngest walkers will become independent learners when they can both find their playthings and return them to the right place.

Identify Problem Spots

You are in and out of your child care space every day and undoubtedly know where most everything can be found, but how long does that take you? Can the children (or anyone else) find what they need or must they ask you? What impression would a visitor or new family have on their first visit to your program? You may think you are organized if *you* know where to find things. That may be acceptable in your personal space, but it simply doesn't work with children. Clutter and disorganization preclude an effective environment and do not support children's learning. In other words, clutter and disorganization have a negative effect on the overall functioning of your program.

Defining the word *clutter* is not easy. I have often been called a "neat freak" (which I take as a compliment) because I function better if I'm not surrounded by unwanted or unused things. Others in my family do not find having many things around them distracting or even define this as clutter.

Clutter is typically defined as a confusing or disorderly state of items. Simply stated, this means many things are disorganized or scattered throughout an identified area. With too much stuff around, adults and children can become frustrated, which in turn can reduce concentration and focus. It's just plain unhealthy and unsafe when too many things are on floors or furniture, or carelessly tucked inside closets and drawers. Clutter can create tripping hazards when the floor is covered with toys, books, or food residue. Outdoor areas littered with things that roll or block play areas can also be tripping hazards. Other kinds of clutter are health hazards. When fabrics are dirty or stored in confined places, dust mites breed easily. Mold and mildew spores grow rapidly from leftover and forgotten food items, and germs and bacteria live on dirty toys handled or mouthed by children. And let's face it, these things simply look bad and often smell bad too.

Most important, clutter is distracting to children's concentration and learning. When children have too many playthings to choose from, they typically choose nothing. When there is too much furniture, children cannot engage in active play or exploration because they are overwhelmed or it's simply too crowded to move. Items hanging from the ceiling become "clutter flutter," and too many wall displays take on the look of highly patterned wallpaper. Instead of supporting children's experiences, cluttered environments prevent learning from happening.

Clutter does not accumulate overnight, so you can't expect to declutter your program space quickly. Creating an organized environment can be downright overwhelming. I'm reminded of the riddle "How can you eat an elephant?" The answer is "One bite at a time." Well, that's exactly what's needed to bring back a feeling of order and organization. Start by removing one small bag or box of unused items from your environment each day.

Start clearing your environment by removing excess furniture, old files, papers, and unnecessary items. This will increase your efficiency. I think you'll be surprised at how this simple process creates

When the environment is cluttered or disorganized, children find making a decision difficult or even frustrating.

an improved workspace that will support a more workable business plan for your FCC program. Less is more in feng shui terms, so simplifying your own space helps you work more efficiently. The following action plan will help you tackle clutter in your child care environment.

1 Make a plan.
   - Start out small—choose only one area.
   - Watch to identify what the children do not use and remove it.
   - Gather storage containers for materials you want to keep and garbage bags for what you're getting rid of.

2 Get to work.
   - Remove items you've identified.
   - Set a timeline for finishing this project.
   - Stay on schedule—play music, dance as you work, sing along with silly songs to make it fun.
   - Involve the children and even family members.
   - Be the Energizer Bunny and keep going.

3 Carry everything to a staging area and sort it into three piles:
   - Items for charity.
   - Items for other providers.
   - Items for the trash can.

4 Be honest as you ask yourself the following:
   - Is this item worth keeping for the children?
   - Will they use it in the future?
   - Does it work?
   - Do I have other learning materials like this that the children use?

5 Clean the area when you've finished removing the clutter.

6 Celebrate your success! If the children have helped with this process, treat them to an extra story, longer outside time, or maybe even bring out some new materials now that you have the space.

7 Repeat this process for all cluttered spaces and ban the "clutterbug" from your child care spaces (and your home).

Stow, Store, or Throw

We once lived next to a man whose living room was a maze formed by stacks of magazines, clothing, boxes, and photographs. He threw out a few things but brought in much. While everything was very orderly (I would almost say neat), it was difficult to move, and no one could do anything in this room. There was simply too much stuff. This is not an uncommon situation for many of us. New things are added to the ones we already have and pretty soon there is no function or organization in the environment. What is needed to keep environments working well is a systematic process I call "Stow, Store, or Throw." These three simple tips can help you organize playthings and keep the environment orderly:

- Stow: Put things away after use.
- Store: Decide what things to remove.
- Throw: Toss or recycle unnecessary items.

STOW

This is something we all learned long ago: there's a place for everything and everything should be in its place. Items kept on shelves should be functional and need to be arranged well to keep them from being visually distracting. Having organized shelves communicates to the children that materials displayed are valued and need to be cared for. Age-appropriate labeling on containers or shelves provides children with predictability and encourages them to use and return materials independently. Use photographs for toddlers and photographs with words for preschoolers and school-age children.

The website of Environments, Inc., (www.eichild .com) includes an easy way to make attractive no-cost labels. Click on "Environments Resources" and open the "Just for Me" Label Maker to make labels for the children's playthings, furniture, or play zones.

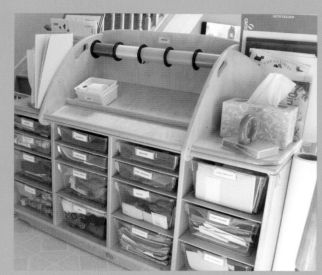

The see-through containers of materials are labeled to help children find and return materials without the provider's assistance. All materials are easy for the children to access.

Labels on these baskets are attached to the handles with shower curtain rings (heavy yarn and chenille stems also work).

Sticky-backed, clear plastic envelopes can be used for labels and are easy to change. (These are sold by office supply stores for storing CD-ROMs or DVDs in folders or notebooks.) Just slip in a photo, apply it to a shelf or box, and you're done. When you rotate materials, put in a different photo to reflect the change.

To get organization and order started, a "must do" first step is to cluster age-appropriate materials, especially those for infants and school-age children, together in one place to help you and the children locate them more easily (chapter 4 offers more ideas). A simple, economical way to organize materials and games within age groups is to cluster them by category or keep them in color-coded bins, boxes, or baskets. For instance, all the dinosaur figures might be kept in the blue container, whereas the cars are stored in the yellow container. Using colors along with labels adds another way to help children locate and return playthings as well as learn classifications, colors, and self-help skills.

Materials on open shelves such as these are easy to find and organize.

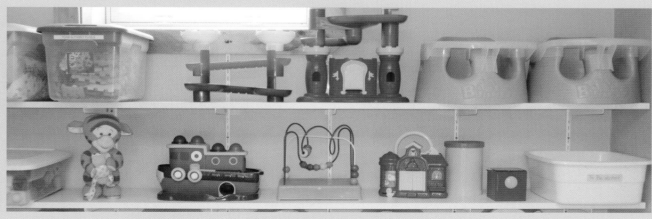

Items in a daily box like this get children excited about what new objects they can explore every day.

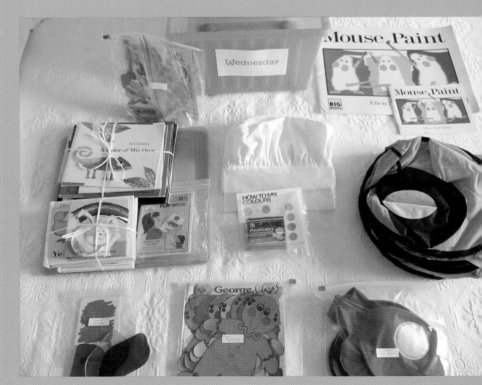

If you have a small child care space that can only hold a small number of materials for each age level, or if you find the children get bored easily with the playthings you have for them, consider rotating some of your materials daily. You can do this by making a "daily box." For example, the "Monday box" has materials brought out only for that day. I used this system when I had my home preschool; the children couldn't wait to see what was in the box each day. Limiting the number of items available and rotating them often helps children find and use materials more easily. Nevertheless, it is important to have a sufficient number and a variety of materials within the children's reach and in the location where they play to support the learning of all the children regardless of their age or ability.

Note that these materials need to *supplement* but not *replace* materials already available to children every day. Items in the daily box should be used only for short periods of time during the day when it becomes apparent that other materials are needed to keep learning happening. At the end of the day, these boxes are put away and stored for use on one day of the following week. Daily box items should be rotated every three to four weeks to keep children excited and eager to use them.

To keep children challenged and enthusiastic about learning with items from the daily box be sure to include a variety of age-appropriate materials for all children in these containers. Use the list below to get started, then change or add other items that reflect the children's interests and abilities.

Items in each box might include the following:

- playdough or "squishy" manipulatives
- one floor puzzle and four or five smaller puzzles
- literature (the number of books depends on the age and number of children—a minimum would be two books per child)
- active play items (including a music CD/DVD for singing, dancing, exercising, and pretending; a parachute; and ribbon wands)
- art/craft materials
- sensory table accessories (for ages two and up)
- two sets of manipulatives for tabletop or floor use
- readiness games/materials (for older toddlers through schoolagers)
- dramatic play accessories (including dress-up items and puppets)

There's an easy method for keeping up with clutter. It's organization—you might even call it micro-organization. Keep empty baskets or bins close by and visible. Have different containers for each category of objects. Keep these containers lightweight and whimsical to encourage children to use them without your help. The task of keeping materials orderly and organized needs to be a joint effort between you and the children.

STORE

Look around to see whether there are items in your child care play space that are not for children's use. Lessen the children's confusion by removing them; there should be no hands-off items anywhere. Everything in the child care space needs to say to the child, "Use me, play with me, and learn from me." To help you decide which materials to remove, make a list of playthings the children use during the day and another list of those they never use. Then ask yourself these questions:

- How long have these materials been out for the children's use?

- Are they age appropriate or developmentally appropriate for the children?

- Can the children see or reach them easily?

- How does the children's play change after more open space is available for the playthings they do use?

The answers to these questions will guide you in changing the environment. While some materials are used daily without children ever losing interest in them, others end up staying on shelves unused day after day. When you notice children are not using materials or are complaining they're bored or "there's nothing to do," it's time to move the materials to another place in the environment or even out the door, or to store them away. For best results, involve the children in this change-out process— it's a great (and inexpensive) way to spark the children's interest in using materials.

When children no longer learn through materials that used to challenge or excite them, it is time to rotate materials. While there is no set schedule for rotating materials (other than watching children as they play), I caution you about making too many changes at one time. If you do not involve the children in making the changes, at least make the changes while they can watch what's happening. This will keep them from being disoriented or disconnected. Remember, children thrive on routine and predictability. Change is good, but too much creates chaos. The environment is only functional when children interact with it.

Now that you have carefully looked at and hopefully removed items from your child care space, it's time to look at your desk or work area. Having well-organized personal and professional materials that are easily available will increase your productivity and may even allow you to be more profitable. Gather your professional resource materials, children's files, U.S. Department of Agriculture (USDA) paperwork, and any other materials related to your child care activities and put them together in one place, for example, a file box, closet shelf, or covered plastic container. Keep these materials out of the children's reach or you may find them decorated with playdough, painted, or cut.

Having adequate room to store materials may be one of your biggest challenges in maintaining an organized child care space. Because most FCC programs have multiage group enrollments, providers must have a mini warehouse of materials appropriate for all ages of children. Finding the right location for storing all these materials is the never-ending challenge. FCC programs typically have three different types of storage needs for materials.

- Temporary: kept in areas that are readily available for use

- Seasonal: kept in areas that can be accessed easily when the children are not in care

- Long-term: kept in areas that take advanced planning to access (such as on high shelves in a garage, storage shed, or rented storage unit)

This well-ordered office closet helps the provider stay organized and productive.

Temporary Storage

Temporary storage is necessary for items that are not used all day or every day but need to be kept in a readily accessible place. If materials are stored where you cannot get to them, they will go unused and be forgotten. Consider your temporary storage as "storage within storage," such as baskets on a shelving unit, or a hanging shoe bag for small items on the back of a closet door. Temporary storage is used daily to keep the balance between your professional and your personal life as you close your business at the end of each day and reopen your home for your family. Taking a few minutes to tuck away child care materials may be the most important of all your storage practices.

The materials in these child care programs can be stored away in these spaces when they are not needed, making the homes welcoming for the providers' own families.

Items you want to store temporarily or for only a short period of time might include children's books, professional resource materials, and arts and crafts materials. These items should be stowed in convenient locations so they are readily available when you need them. One provider stored all her daily supplies on a rolling kitchen cart kept in a closet where it was out of sight and reach by her family, but was quickly accessible when needed for child care activities.

Additional temporary storage locations can be found under a bed or sofa, behind a large piece of furniture (for example, a sofa or an entertainment center), in a nearby closet, or in a cabinet or storage unit.

A kitchen cart or an old suitcase can be loaded with exciting learning materials and moved to areas where they are needed. When not in use, they can be stowed away in a temporary storage location.

Furniture and toys find a new home hiding behind this sofa after the child care children leave for the day.

Wicker baskets are functional storage containers for children's personal belongings. This provider uses detachable and easy-to-change name tags on each basket.

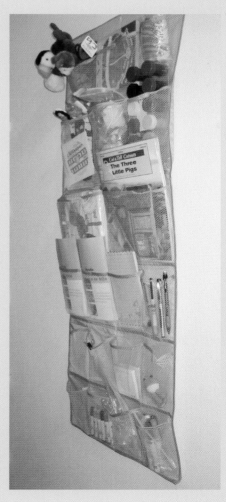

This hanging organizer provides great storage for art supplies or other small materials.

Plastic storage containers are easy to clean and can be easily toted around by children.

Many types of containers are sold just for storage, but you can use any number of other containers, such as the following:

- shoe boxes
- plastic jars
- fishing tackle boxes
- garden tool totes
- suitcases and tote bags (with wheels)
- laundry bags with drawstrings
- plastic cleaning supply totes
- cloth conference bags (especially zippered ones)
- cutlery trays
- empty coffee cans (cover sharp edges!)

By keeping all materials nearby, these storage containers make any performance effortless.

Most closets are designed for hanging clothes and so have few shelves. To create storage space that can be hidden behind a closed door, remove the rod for hanging clothes and add more shelves. If you have a large closet in your child care space, add a dresser to hold temporary storage items. Keep the closet doors open and encourage the children to use and return playthings kept inside of labeled drawers. Either way, investing in added shelving is probably the best solution to maximize closet space—you can more than double the storage. Some providers like wooden shelves, whereas others prefer the metal slatted shelving systems sold at home improvement centers and discount stores. Components of these systems include poles, shelves, cabinets, stacking drawers, wire baskets, and hooks. Such storage systems come with instructions and are often easy to install yourself. I like them because they can be rearranged and pieces can be added or removed to suit specific needs.

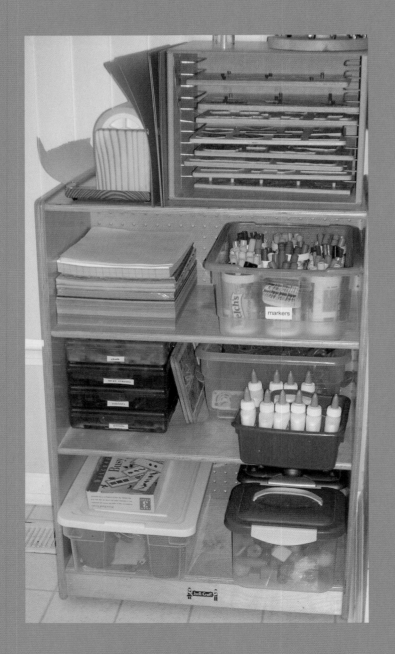

When arranging components for messy activities and activities with small pieces, different shelving options like these can lessen the headache of organizing.

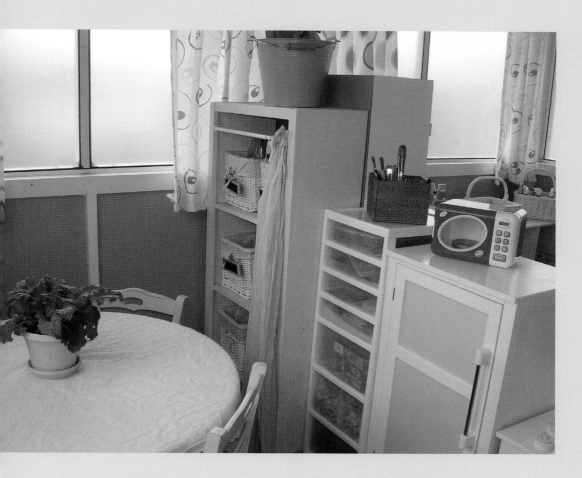

These organized and labeled shelving units can be easily accessed by children in the dramatic play area.

Shelving and small chests of drawers can maximize the storage space in any closet.

Seasonal Storage

Seasonal materials are items you use yearly for short periods of time. Besides holiday materials, they include items used only during spring, summer, fall, or winter. Some examples are beach balls, sleds, music tapes or CDs, books, and dramatic play props. Sort, label, and store these by theme in bags or boxes in a location away from your child care space, for example, in a basement, garage, or storage shed. Clear containers allow you to see at a glance exactly which items are in each container. If you use cardboard boxes, consider inviting the children to draw or paint pictures indicating what's stored inside. Old suitcases are great for storing seasonal items. Children get so excited when suitcases are brought out—they may have stories to tell about vacations, trips to see grandparents, or family seasonal activities.

Labeled storage containers make preparing for new activities much easier.

Long-Term Storage

It may be necessary to own some items, but you may not need them for a long period of time, or the items may be too large to leave out when you're not using them. Examples include age-appropriate materials such as high chairs, portable cribs, roller skates, or board games that are needed only when you have children of a particular age enrolled in your program. Store these items in a remote but accessible area such as the attic, the back of a storage shed, or a top shelf in the garage. You might want to coordinate with other providers to set up a lending library for seldom-needed or seldom-used items. This is cost effective and will greatly reduce the need for bulky long-term storage items. Some providers rent a small storage unit just for big or seldom-used items.

THROW

While you never throw away anything until you're ready, this simple rule will help: when one new item comes in, one old item goes out (unless you are trying to grow your inventory of materials). Keep only the items you really need or love or that have great value. I still have a lesson plan book from my first year of teaching and simply can't give it up. Here are a few ways to get items out of your sight and, ultimately, out of your home:

- If you belong to a local FCC association, consider having a quarterly recycling event to get rid of all those annoying things just lying around your house that are unused or "unloved." Take a few minutes to load up a recycling bin, box, or heavy-duty plastic bag with treasures you no longer want. Bring them to swap with fellow providers. One provider's junk may be another provider's treasure.

- Donate give-away items to homeless shelters, doctor or dentist offices, hospitals, or church nurseries, where clean, gently used playthings are always needed.

- Throwing items away may be the right thing to do if the materials have been overly loved or used, look old or beat-up, or smell so bad that no one else wants them either!

Storage areas that are clean and free of clutter make it easier for children to find items they want.

To keep your surroundings organized with minimal effort, do a clean sweep each night before you turn out the light or close the door to your child care space. As you accumulate new items, stay organized by regularly donating and tossing things you no longer use. If you have a much-loved item you simply cannot part with, consider storing it away. Also, be sure each item has a home, so you and the children can put things away quickly and find them easily.

Rotate Materials

Sometimes as I observe children at play, I notice they are roaming in the environment—they never seem to be involved with peers or materials. These grazers move from one place to another looking for something that interests them, and when they don't find anything they simply move on to another place. Just as children outgrow their clothes, they outgrow materials and equipment. When they no longer learn through the environment, it's time for change. The environment is only functional and exciting when children interact with it. Otherwise, it is much like a museum—just a nice display of unused materials in one place.

How long do you keep materials out for children's use? As long as the materials are interesting to the children and they learn by using them. Open-ended toys such as blocks, cars and trucks, toy animals, and Lego blocks are flexible enough to be used in varying ways. Typically, these favorite traditional toys are used continuously and are effective learning tools for children of all ages. Rotating (or removing) materials is needed only when children do not use them or tell you they are "boring" or "there's nothing to do." My rule of thumb has always been that when you see dust or cobwebs on materials, it's time to change them for new ones.

Changing too much too quickly is unsettling to young children, so be careful about how many materials you remove and replace at one time. To keep confusion and disorientation to a minimum, involve children in the process. Remember, children thrive on routine and predictability. Change is good, but too much change can create chaos.

Keep materials you intend to rotate in accessible containers, for example, clear plastic containers with lids, clear zippered or ziplock bags, or sturdy plastic bags that are tagged to show their contents. Pay a few pennies more and buy the most durable storage containers available. They should last longer and are a better value.

Keep an Inventory

When you think about how to inventory materials you have on hand for your program, think about how you buy ingredients for a recipe. You check what you already have. Why would you buy another bag of sugar when you already have one? It would be a waste of money. Think of the different categories of materials for varying ages of children as staples for a recipe. Keeping an accurate inventory list is time well spent. Having an accurate list becomes essential when you have the funds or need to add more materials to your program.

Keep your inventory list current and be sure to indicate the location of the materials, for example, "large garbage bag stored on top shelf in garage" or "plastic container marked Summer Toys." When this is done, locating materials and putting them in your environment for the children to use will be much easier. Use the Materials Inventory table in appendix E to help you determine what you have and what you need.

Keep the Problem Solved

A functional learning environment helps to ensure a fun and safe place for you and the children. When clutter is minimized, safety and health practices increase and fire hazards decrease. All in all, less clutter means your well-organized environment will be a place of busy, happy, and (probably) noisy learners every day. In fact, decluttering the environment is so important to children's learning that Elena Giacopini (1997) suggests a well-organized space is like having another adult to help children.

The following sets of photographs show before and after scenes from real FCC providers. These providers worked systemically through their clutter and, with help from the older children (preschoolers and up), cleaned up the clutter and kept it gone. I know it's difficult to believe these are the same spaces but through patience, persistence, and cooperation, clutter is gone and order has been restored.

Before

After

Before

After

The comment I hear most often about clutter is "I can't keep up with clutter, and it (the environment) looks so disorganized." I agree. It seems clutter has a life of its own and grows over time. An easy answer to this problem is, of course, organization. I am a big believer in teaching children early in life to be responsible for themselves—and that includes cleaning up after they play. Remind children to put away materials right after they use them. Have different containers for each category of objects. For example, musical instruments might go into a big basket, while dramatic play clothes are hung in the housekeeping zone. Keep lightweight baskets, storage bins, and decorative empty boxes close by and visible. Look for containers that are unusual or whimsical to encourage children to use them without your help.

○ ○ ○

This chapter stressed the importance of keeping child care spaces free of clutter to promote children's learning. Organization helps children find, use, and return materials easily and independently. Materials that are well cared for tell children those items are valued and should not be abused. Items that are used together should be kept together. To help you remember what you have on hand and what you still need, develop and keep an inventory of all your materials and where they are stored.

Chapter 4 presents ways to help you remove the institutional look from your home child care spaces. You'll find many no-cost or low-cost ways to put "home" back into your child care program, not as a decorator, but as an educator.

Activities and Questions

To get a better grasp of how to organize and declutter the environment, go into your child care space as you consider the following questions:

1   Where does clutter accumulate in your child care environment (or in your house) and what can you do to organize those spaces?

2   Locate places for temporary, short-term, and long-term storage. If the storage areas you identified are already full, could they be cleared out? (Just a note of caution here: be sensitive to your family members' needs too!)

3   What types of storage containers for small items (books, puzzles, arts/crafts materials, and dramatic play accessories) would make the environment appear less cluttered?

4   Look for dead space, for example, behind furniture, under sofas or beds, or on the backs of closet doors, to use for storage. What items can you store there for easy access when you need them?

5   Organize a Recycle Day or a Swap Shop with fellow providers at an upcoming association training or event. Only items in good working order, complete, and safe should be traded.

6   Use the feng shui principle that children need order and structure to support their learning. To help children learn to respect materials, always put items away after use, and keep the environment clutter-free. (Trust me on this one—it will bring an amazingly positive change into your entire home.)

Putting the "Home" in Home Child Care

The environment around us affects our daily living. The feeling or atmosphere of a place sets the stage for the activities and interactions that occur there and for how people engage in those activities. Libraries and art museums are places of reflection and thinking. Bowling alleys and playgrounds are places of noise and fun. Learning places for young children should be comfortable and homelike. Children need environments that accommodate their different moods and activities and welcome them in. Homestyle environments must be designed to be functional, organized, and efficient to meet the learning needs of children through play and exploration.

This chapter considers indoor design elements and helps you put them together to create the ideal homelike family child care environment.

> Homestyle environments meet the needs of children through exciting learning places and spaces where they feel comfortable and a sense of belonging.
>
> —LINDA GEIGLE

Offering plenty of activities and comfortable elements, this homestyle living room is inviting for both child and adult.

This child care space is warm and welcoming for children and complements the other areas of the provider's home. Uncovered windows flood the room with natural light.

Homestyle Spaces

Recently, I visited an FCC program where I really felt the feeling of home everywhere I looked. Children sat on a quilt-covered sofa and read books they found in a large wicker basket on the coffee table. They ate at the kitchen table, which had been fitted with booster seats for the littlest ones. Containers and baskets full of homemade or gently used materials were placed on small rug samples to designate where they were to be used. The dining room table was draped with tenting and, when I peeked inside, I found a backpack full of camping gear for a creative playtime experience. I felt at home, and after watching the children for a short time, it was evident that this homestyle environment was supporting their learning.

This chapter describes *zones* rather than interest centers or interest areas because, due to space limitations and the multiage enrollment in FCC programs, the child care space is used for a variety of purposes. The area for large group activities is also the area for music and movement and the area for quiet relaxation is also the library nook. This is explained in more detail later in this chapter.

The design of this large child care space is based on the children's needs and keeps them interested and involved. Children can move freely between three interconnected rooms and, using carefully placed mirrors, the provider can maintain line-of-sight supervision at all times.

This small child care room is used for imaginative play only. Since the floor space is limited, the provider has used labeled storage pieces to help children find and return materials easily.

This cozy place uses a crib mattress against the wall. By adding a crib bumper pad, it quickly changes into a safe sleeping space whenever needed.

In these semi-enclosed areas, a child can be alone or with just a few friends.

These areas that are separated from active play help children slow down, relax, and enjoy a quiet time during a busy day.

The space has been arranged so children can choose from a variety of materials throughout the room. Children play in these areas without being crowded, and materials are organized to help them work and play independently.

Room Arrangements

The preceding chapters have outlined essential components for child care spaces that support children's learning. Keep these design basics in mind as you start planning and creating environments that are not only homelike and pleasing to the eye, but also functional and practical. Think long and hard about how each space will actually be used. How much play or project work will go on there? What ages and how many children will want to use each space at one time? Don't forget to include a separate place for older children to "get away" or for infants to be safe and cozy. Once you have considered all the basics, you are ready to start the fun part—the design.

Use the following steps and the grid in appendix D to help you create exciting and welcoming environments in your child care spaces. A printable version of the grid is available at Redleaf Press's website (www.redleafpress .org) on the *Family Child Care Homes* product page. Make multiple copies of the grid. You will need at least one for each room where you are licensed for child care. Use it to help revise a current room arrangement in your home that has many "warning signs" (not supporting children's learning) or to create an additional or a new room environment. Information included later in this chapter explains how zones can be in different rooms of your home (in fact, for most children, having opportunities to move from room to room keeps learning fresh and fun).

STEP ONE: MEASURE YOUR SPACE

Measure the room's length and width from wall to wall using a tape measure. Be sure the entire length of your tape measure is parallel to the floor. Use your measurements for step two.

STEP TWO: DRAW YOUR SPACE

Sketch the room dimensions on the room grid. Each grid square represents one foot (12 inches) in the room. Draw to size all permanent or immovable elements within the room such as closets, cabinets, sinks, and built-in bookshelves.

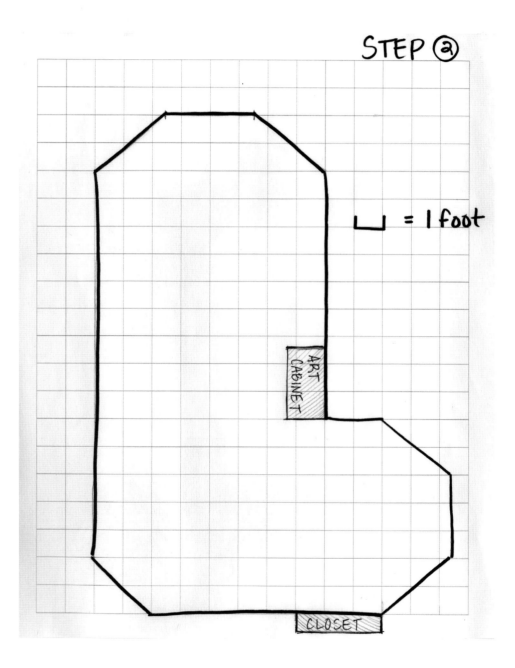

STEP ②

⌐⌐ = 1 foot

ART CABINET

CLOSET

STEP THREE: DEFINE YOUR SPACE

Mark the location of the following room elements:

- Doors: note whether these swing into or out of the room.

- Windows: note the height from the floor if a piece of furniture is in front of the window.

- Electricity: note with an "E" where each outlet is located; use an "S" for each light switch.

- Heating or air conditioning vents: note with a "V."

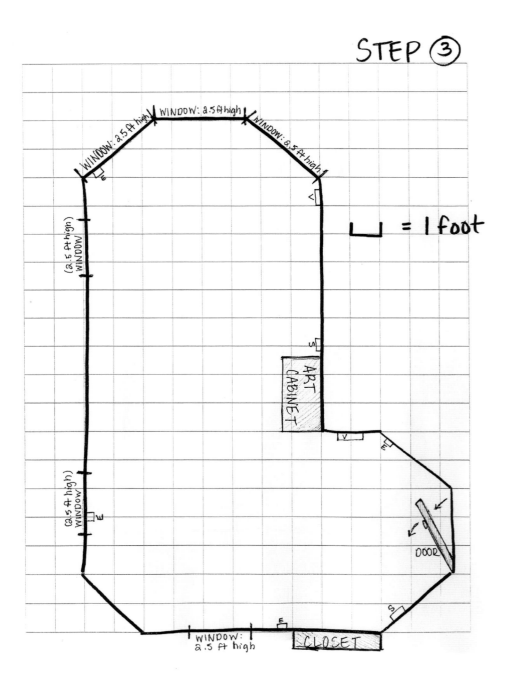

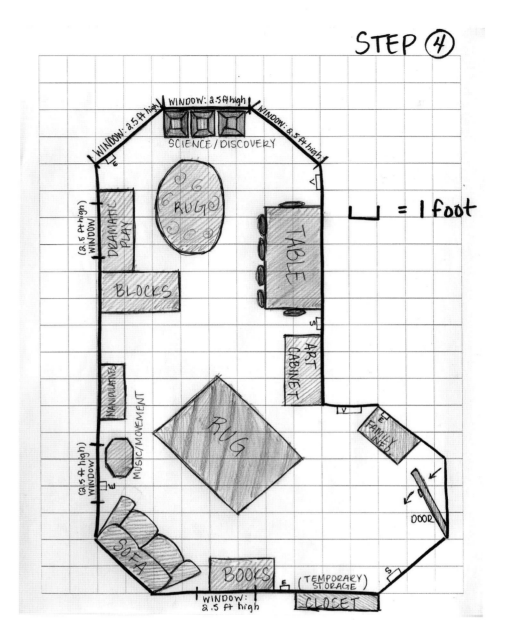

STEP ④

WINDOW: 2.5 ft high
WINDOW: 2.5 ft high
WINDOW: 2.5 ft high

SCIENCE / DISCOVERY

RUG

(2.5 ft high) WINDOW

DRAMATIC PLAY

TABLE

⌐⌐ = 1 foot

BLOCKS

MANIPULATES

MUSIC / MOVEMENT

(2.5 ft high) WINDOW

ART CABINET

RUG

FAMILY FARNED

SOFA

DOOR

BOOKS

(TEMPORARY) STORAGE

CLOSET

WINDOW: 2.5 ft high

STEP FOUR: DESIGN YOUR SPACE

Draw in a piece of furniture or an area rug. Then add activity zones around the walls, always keeping in mind the activities planned for this room. Leave some space open for pathways and physical play. A good rule of thumb is to have furniture in approximately half the room and the other half open. You may want to make furniture templates drawn to the same scale as the grid sheet (one grid square for each twelve inches). Moving these paper pieces around on the room grid is much easier and quicker than erasing or creating multiple sheets for each room (or moving pieces of furniture or large rugs in the room itself!).

Ask yourself the following questions:

- Are learning zones included that reflect the children's ages, abilities, and interests?
- Are there places for children to play as a group? By themselves?
- What "grab 'n' go" (movable or portable) learning zones are in this room?
- Where is the accessible storage to support activities in this room?
- Are there clear pathways to encourage children to move from place to place and safely to the exit door?
- Is the room environment functional, organized, and safe?
- Are there open spaces to keep the children from being overcrowded?
- Will the environment encourage children to interact with the materials and with each other?
- Will the environment support children as independent learners?
- Does the space arrangement incorporate overlapping learning zones to support the children's integrated learning experiences (such as music with language arts, fine-motor with readiness or creativity, gross-motor with social skill development)?
- Can the room environment be changed easily as the enrollment changes?

STEP FIVE: MOVE INTO THE SPACE

Now it's time to move into the room using your completed room grid sheet as a guide. Look critically at lighting, ventilation, electrical outlets, and storage as you place furniture. Think of textures, colors, smells, sounds, and the homestyle feeling of the room. Include enough materials to support children's play and learning, but not so many that children may be overwhelmed or the area becomes too crowded or cluttered. When you're convinced you have a functional arrangement, add details such as lamps, open baskets of materials, pillows, and meaningful wall displays.

I knew a provider who planned her child care spaces for weeks, first drawing everything on grid paper and then using catalog pictures to be sure everything looked just right. She called me to ask for help because what looked functional on paper did not work out as she'd planned once everything was in place. Here are a few things to think about should this happen to you:

- Find something that is functional in the space and retain that as a starting point.

- Put everything else in the center of the room or remove it all.

- Think like children do—would they know what should happen in each place? Is the furniture size appropriate for them?

- Reshape the room arrangement gradually, bringing back only the purposeful and age-appropriate materials you know children will use.

- Ensure that all the furniture is not against walls, thus creating an overly large zone in the middle of the room. (Some children feel smaller and less confident in large spaces, whereas others tend to run and chase in spaces that are "too big.")

- Is there an overabundance of furniture creating smaller alcoves or "nests" that cause children to become overly crowded?

- Can you see everywhere in the room, or are there areas where tall furniture or dividers keep you from maintaining line-of-sight supervision?

STEP SIX: PLAY IN THE SPACE

Yes, that's right. Get down on your knees and move from area to area within the room to get a child's perspective of the environment. Stop a while to play in each zone just as the children will. Although you cannot predict how the children will interact in this room, looking at the environment through their eyes will give you a better idea of whether this space invites and welcomes them to explore and learn. If the physical environment doesn't seem inviting as you are moving within it, take a few photographs from the children's eye level. As you study them, keep in mind that children need to be connected to the environment and have a sense of belonging for it to be effective. Redesign or recreate your space by thinking like a child.

Putting It All Together

Except for hotel rooms and motor homes, I'm aware of no standardized environment design—certainly none for children's learning environments. Our houses are all different to meet the needs and personalities of our families within the amount of space our houses provide. Likewise, there is no standard design guide you can follow for your child care practice. As you create your layout, keep in mind a basic plan that will give more and better purpose to the space. Of course, there also must be flexibility based on the needs, ages, and number of children whose learning will be affected by this physical environment. Develop a strategy using zones that are designed to answer the question "What happens here?" Consider the following as you arrange the environment:

- traffic flow and open pathways that do not disturb ongoing activities
- the activity and noise levels associated with the activities in each zone
- lighting convenience
- the number of items needed to support the activities in each zone
- how readily accessible stored items are
- the learning goal or purpose of each zone

An effective family child care environment can be designed in many ways. Arranging and rearranging a room on paper is much easier than moving heavy furniture from place to place.

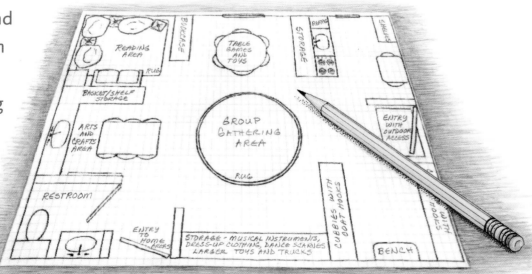

Much like a city planner who designs roads to accommodate the number of cars using them, shops and buildings based on the needs of the community, and sidewalks where pedestrians need them, you can think of the overall physical arrangement of your space as a collection of places and pathways. With too many pathways, there are no places to go—but with too few pathways, there is no way to get from one place to another. As you put it all together, consider the following items for each zone:

Entryway
- sign in/out area
- place for child's belongings
- family information area

Work Zone
- tables and chairs appropriately sized for the children involved
- open display of materials (such as shelves, see-through containers, and baskets)
- a variety of easy-to-clean work surfaces for
  - creative arts
  - manipulatives
  - writing readiness
  - games and puzzles
  - cooking and eating
  - exploration and discovery

Large-Space Zone
- a large open space
- open-ended materials to support
  - music
  - movement and dance
  - physical games
  - dramatic play and productions

Quiet or Comfy Zone

- pillows (only for children over twelve months old)
- a bean bag chair (check manufacturer/licensing restrictions for use with children under three years), sofa, or upholstered chair
- a textured rug or a carpeted area
- bookshelves or open baskets with age-appropriate children's books

Messy or Active Play Zone

- a messy play area near a water source or bathroom with equipment or furnishings to support
  - painting
  - cooking
  - science experiments
  - sensory play (such as water and sand)
- an active play area with open shelves of materials to support
  - construction
  - block play

Alone Zone

- a room for a single child or two or three children to
  - have time to decompress
  - be by themselves
  - feel welcomed, not punished
- a protected area (a corner is ideal)
- a small rug, pillows
- a ceiling drop-over area (see-through netting, a fabric swag, a kite)
- a semi-enclosed structure with a clear line of sight inside (such as a small tent or a cutaway appliance box)

Imagination Zone

- dramatic play props
- a "pretend area"
- puppets
- a flannel board

Learning zones in FCC programs are fluid. They can be combined or portable according to the size of your child care space and the needs and interests of the children. The most important part of the process is setting up an environment where children want to be and stay to learn. The key elements for designing learning zones in your FCC program are listed below. Each zone should have the following:

- a variety of exciting age-appropriate materials or activities
- open-ended materials or activities that support discovery and learning for children of all ages and abilities
- an environment that is orderly and organized to help children be independent learners
- materials and activities that are rotated when children appear to be disinterested or do not use the items

Provider Krissy LaPorte summed up the process in these words: "The biggest challenge in setting up my child care space has been finding the right balance between allowing my home to be a reflection of my own personal style and incorporating day care materials that not only suit the children's individual needs but also allow them to feel warm and welcome. Having the children feel like they are entering their home-away-from-home has always been my goal. What I have learned is that much of this can be achieved from the first hug they receive when they walk through the door. Meeting them at eye level, displaying photos of them and their artwork, and providing a place for their own special things are also things I do to help them feel at home."

As you create elements in your child care space, always keep in mind that the feeling of the environment should be

- safe
- homelike
- happy!
- soft and comfortable
- inviting
- a celebration of diversity

What children experience with their senses influences how they feel and learn within an environment. To that end, the environment should also have these characteristics:

- be orderly and organized
- be clean and shiny
- be free of clutter and have a limited number of patterns
- have a comfortable sound level
- include texture to help children explore through touch
- be full of happy faces and pleasant sounds

FOOD ZONES

Mealtime is an important time for young children to talk, laugh, and share the same foods with their friends and you around a table. These are both nourishing and nurturing times for children, as well as an important part of the family child care environment. Promoting good health and nutrition for children in family child care is crucial, so the food they consume while there is equally important. Creating a fun and relaxing mealtime environment encourages children with self-help skills (using utensils), decision-making skills (what and how much to eat), and social skills (talking and listening with others). Some quick and easy ways to set the scene for a peaceful mealtime environment include the following:

- Play soft, relaxing music.
- Use contrast between the color of food and the color of plates and cups (children make food choices first with their eyes).
- To keep distractions down, avoid patterned plates and tablecloths.
- Include mouth-watering smells in your eating area to increase children's appetites.
- Laugh, talk, eat, and enjoy each other's company!
- Clear the table of all items not associated with mealtime.
- Set up consistent places to sit at the table (some children like "reserved seating").
- Create interesting table centerpieces (our grandson calls these "masterpieces," which I think is a great term).
- Enjoy a meal or snack in a safe but fun alternative location, such as on a blanket *under* the table, under a blossoming tree, on the circle time rug, or near the backyard fence.

With a clear table, an attractive decoration, and name cards at their seats, the children's meals and snacks are peaceful, organized, and enjoyable.

Creating an Environment to Celebrate Differences

One day when I was the director of an Army child development center, children in a toddler room were helping me unpack a box of newly arrived materials. As the multicultural dolls were being unwrapped, one of the toddlers starting giving them out to her friends. She looked carefully at each doll and then gave it to a child whose race or gender was the same as the doll. Studies have shown that children begin noticing racial differences in their infancy (Kelly et al. 2007) and that by the age of three or four, their understanding of race is fairly well established (Steele, Choi, and Ambady 2004). Young children are observant. They see differences in people with disabilities and know that some people are rich or poor, old or young. Learning environments must help children with the following concepts:

- learning that people can be different yet still have much in common
- feeling great about themselves
- celebrating their own family's unique characteristics
- being respectful of others who are different from them

Creating an environment to help children understand likenesses and differences in people must start with the children themselves. A "tourist approach" environment with posters from foreign countries, American Indian feather headdresses, or sombreros in the dramatic play zone do little to help children connect themselves with other races or cultures (Saul and Saul 2001).

These two girls are playing with items from a basket of multicultural materials.

To create an environment that celebrates differences, start by learning about each child in your care. Be careful when making assumptions about a child's family. Many young children live in family units with only one parent, with grandparents, or with gay or lesbian parents. Part of your intake interview should include asking about family traditions, holiday celebrations, family members, family cultural background, and favorite foods. Also, consider each child's interests and questions. This will tell you what a child knows and wants to know about people from differing backgrounds.

Wall displays are a great way to share the specific traits of each family. A wall display can include items such as:

- a photo collage of the children and their families, their homes, and extended family members

- a family heritage quilt with a square made by each family out of fabric or memorabilia significant to them (add squares as new families come into your program)

- "all about town" photos showing people in your neighborhood, community, city, or state in nonstereotypic ways, for example, a female doctor, a male preschool teacher, or an older female bus driver

- commercial pictures of foreign countries that are of significance to the children and that portray the "everyday culture" of homes and cities and the typical activities of children and families

- a world map indicating the cultural background of each family, including yours

- an art print from a famous artist that depicts a landscape or region that is different from where you and the children live

Include books about children with special needs, diverse family units, or intergenerational characters doing normal, everyday activities. Reading folktales, fairytales, and fables from around the world is another way to share and celebrate diversity. You also can include recorded music, instruments, toy foods, empty clean boxes of real foods, and cooking/eating utensils from many cultures. Share and celebrate the diversity of the children and families in your care through play and discovery using these items:

- Natural elements: rocks, seashells, sand, and photos of plants and bodies of water from families' trips or homelands

- Food: ask family members for recipes you can make and serve at mealtime

- Math and numbers: abacus, marbles, games, and decks of playing cards from other countries

- Manipulatives: puzzles, small multicultural family and intergenerational figures and dolls, small toy animals

- Families' baskets: made using items families have contributed to share their heritage, culture, traditions, or celebrations

- Dress-up items: child-sized costumes or dolls in costume from around the world (NOTE: If you provide these props in your environment, be sure to tell the children that such clothing is worn only on special occasions, not every day. When we moved to Spain, one of our daughter's biggest shocks was that little girls did not wear flamenco dresses to school every day as she had seen in books.)

It is important to remind children of how children around the world are more alike than different from them, including in how they dress. Many multicultural dolls are dressed in traditional clothing that typically is not worn every day.

CELEBRATING HOLIDAYS

Children love and look forward to holidays and the fun that goes along with each one. I lived overseas for almost thirty years and during that time had some wonderful experiences sharing my family's holiday traditions and learning about those celebrated in the countries where I lived. The goal in your program should be to have respect for everyone's customs. Holidays are perfect opportunities for children and families to share their traditions. A quick written survey of families asking about their traditions, celebrations, and religious or cultural beliefs (which might keep children from participating in your holiday activities) should be done annually and kept on file for planning purposes. By planning together with families, you can decide how to celebrate and create a festive environment that is meaningful to the children and comfortable for their families.

Children must value and connect to a holiday for it to be meaningful. Above all, resist creating a holiday environment that is overly stimulating. An environment with twinkly lights, sparkly mobiles from the ceiling, or overly commercialized displays may be cute, but it is devoid of meaning or learning value. Ask families to bring in memorabilia to display, such as photos of past family celebrations, favorite holiday books, easy holiday recipes or foods, or arts and crafts projects. All these will encourage connections between families as well as promote respect and understanding of diverse celebrations for the children.

Sometimes all families in family child care programs have similar ethnicities, religions, or cultures. If this is true of your enrollment, and with permission from the families, look to your immediate community to include additional cultural or religious holiday celebrations of families and children from different backgrounds. You also can connect the children in your care with the larger community by displaying photos or posters of community celebrations or holiday activities, inviting a guest speaker, or sharing home-made gifts or cards with children who are not part of their culture. Such activities help children understand that holiday customs are celebrated in many ways and, just as they enjoy their celebration, children from other backgrounds enjoy their celebrations too.

Design for Children with Special Needs

A few years ago I visited an FCC home where a child with severe physical disabilities was enrolled. Although the provider's care for typically developing children was high quality, her home did not support the child with special needs. The doorways were not wide enough for his wheelchair, so he had to be carried into the house and to the bathroom. Playthings and books were located out of his reach, and no playground equipment was appropriate for his use. All the other children were independent learners, that is, they could get to all the materials they saw. Sadly, this child had to wait for help or, if no one assisted him, simply watch as the others played.

Caring for children with special needs has been one of the most rewarding experiences of my career. Their needs are great but so is their love. Families of children with special needs have indicated that finding child care is one of their most difficult struggles. Although providers continue to tell me they want to care for these children, their child care environment simply cannot support the various needs children with disabilities may have.

Federal laws Titles II and III of the Americans with Disabilities Act (ADA) of 1990 and Section 504 of the Rehabilitation Act of 1973 set guidelines for child care programs for enrollment of children with disabilities. The basic environmental provisions include *reasonable modification* to child care facilities, including homes. "Reasonable modifications or accommodations" means making needed changes to help a child with special needs reach her potential. For example, this may mean having ramps or handrails to help a child with limited mobility, or large-print books for a child with limited eyesight, or large-piece puzzles for a child with limited fine-motor skills. I once taught a child who needed "reserved seating" close to me to help him focus and learn. This was his reasonable accommodation. The typically developing children (children without diagnosed disabilities) do not require any modification or accommodation to help them learn. However, if an accommodation is taken away from a child with an identified condition, that child cannot be a successful learner.

Title III of the ADA specifies basic requirements for all programs caring for children outside of their homes, including schools, child care centers, and FCC programs. The guidelines require you to provide the same opportunities for children—those with and those without special needs—to participate in your program. Assistance in interpreting ADA guidelines is available free of charge from the U.S. Department of Justice (800-514-0301 or www .ada.gov/childq&a.htm). Some of the most important guidelines pertaining to you as a family child care provider include the following:

This family child care home provides easy access for a child in a wheelchair so he can join activities with his friends.

- Children with special needs must have an equal opportunity to be enrolled and then to freely participate in quality child care programs.

- The home where you provide child care must have adequate modifications to ensure the safety of children with special needs while they're in your home and must support their learning success.

- Tax credits (up to $5,000 per year) and tax deductions (up to $15,000 per year) are available for small businesses to offset the cost of making needed changes to comply with the ADA. Do not assume your home cannot support a child's special needs without major and costly changes.

When you have a child with disabilities enrolled in your program, ensure that you have an open line of communication with the family so you can provide those modifications their child needs. They are your best source of guidance, so feel free to ask them as many questions as you need. Environmental modifications must be determined on a child-by-child basis; don't jump to conclusions based on what others might have told you. In addition to the child's family, other resources are available to you through local, state, or federal government agencies. They will help you make changes, so don't feel you need to do this alone. Ask for help—it's there and it's free.

Every child has a special "wonderfulness"—his smile, her sloppy kisses, the way she laughs or runs or sings. Children with special needs deserve the same quality care as is provided to typically developing children. A diagnosis of disability describes only limitations, not potential. Like all children, children with disabilities need a physical environment that invites them in. They also need a social-emotional environment where they feel a sense of belonging. Above all, they need your support. This takes more than a checklist or regulatory guidelines. It takes your commitment to address the needs of a child with disabilities. When you are committed, your environment will have a positive effect on *all* children in your program.

Selecting Furniture and Playthings

Furnishings in our homes frame our personality, our family's needs, and the feeling we want our homes to have. I work from home and have a homestyle office. It has everything I need to run a business: a computer, a filing cabinet, a phone, and a fax machine; it does not have business-style furnishings such as a metal desk, plastic chairs, portable cubicle dividers, or a large copy machine. I want my home business to be as much *home* as it is *business*.

These same guidelines apply when picking out furnishings for child care environments that are part of a home. Family child care is a home-based business, but often the word "home" is left out of the picture. If photos were taken of your child care environment, would the viewer know it's a part of your home, or does it have an institutional feeling? Both the children in your care and your family members benefit from being surrounded by the comforts of a homestyle environment.

The members of your family are an important part of your FCC program. Meeting your family's needs when your program is not open is critical, for they live in the home where you operate your business. Furnishings must appeal to your family members as well as meet the needs of your program. The following pages deal with things to consider when you choose furnishings.

Selecting furniture to fit both business needs
and your own personality can be challenging.
This office uses homestyle furnishings that
complement the home's décor and are
appropriate for a child care business.

These providers
store away business
materials while their
programs are not
operational.

QUALITY AND SAFETY

Manufacturing safety guidelines for children's furniture are limited to cribs, bunk beds, high chairs, and some materials used for construction and finishes (U.S. Congress 2008; Consumer Product Safety Commission 2010). The manufacturing of other children's furniture, such as tables and chairs or shelving units and cubbies, is unregulated by governmental standards. These other pieces of furniture come in all styles and are made from many different materials. Sturdiness is a major consideration, since children use furniture in all kinds of unintended ways (and you never know when you'll be asked to sit with them for a tea party or a puppet show).

PERSONAL PREFERENCE

Ask your family members for their help and suggestions in choosing furnishings. Look at the rest of your home and choose furnishings that are similar in style.

DOUBLE DUTY

Look for furnishings that meet the needs of your family and the children in your program, such as coffee tables with big drawers for storage, low shelving units that fold and close, or area rugs that blend with the room's décor.

VENDORS AND MANUFACTURERS

Think beyond suppliers who sell institutional style furnishings for center-based programs and schools. Rather than purchasing furnishings that look institutional, find things that are durable and safe but have a feeling of home. Quality homestyle children's furniture is available from many sources and is very appropriate for FCC programs. Use the Materials Inventory table in appendix E as well as the buying guidelines that follow to help you choose furnishings that are appropriate for the size and ages of children in your care.

Here are ten tips to help you select furnishings and playthings for learning zones:

1   Choose only safe, durable, washable items free of small parts that can cause choking.

2   Make a budget and stick to it.

3   Start with the basics and add optional materials later.

4   Purchase multipurpose, unstructured materials that can be used for a variety of play experiences for children of many age levels.

5   Select materials that support total child development, for example, motor skills, social-emotional growth, creativity and imagination, discovery and exploration, language and literacy.

6   Be especially aware of space limitations in your home when selecting furniture.

7   Look for items that take child power, not batteries, to make them work.

8   Remember that less-defined toys and multiuse furniture help children use their imagination more.

9   Check the recommended ages for playthings to ensure they are age appropriate.

10 Keep in mind that award winners are not always better toys (check to see who gave the award and why—many times manufacturers give out their own awards).

Preferred Shelving Dimensions for Children

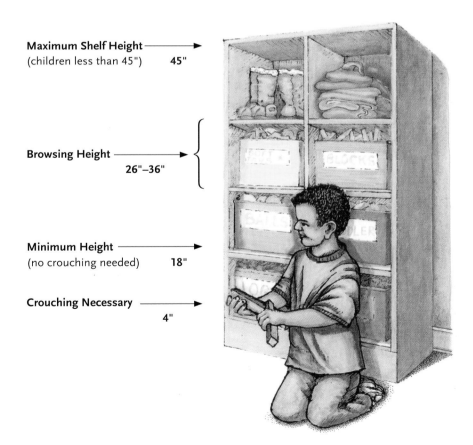

Maximum Shelf Height (children less than 45") **45"**

Browsing Height **26"–36"**

Minimum Height (no crouching needed) **18"**

Crouching Necessary **4"**

Playthings (or toys) are tools children use to learn. Appropriate and challenging toys are the tools children use to influence their play and make their young years count. Playthings range from old pots and refrigerator boxes to expensive toys, games, and puzzles. Toys that engage young children help them learn life skills such as being creative, developing self-esteem, and knowing how to cooperate. Providing a balance of materials to accommodate all the children's needs can be overwhelming. Use the following criteria as you select materials for your child care environment. Materials should have the following characteristics:

- age appropriate
- safe and free of small parts that can cause choking
- durable and free of breakable parts
- useful for teaching more than one skill or concept
- stimulating to the senses (colorful, textural, even noisy)
- easily stored
- supportive of the development of children's skills
- conducive to extending play rather than limiting it
- able to promote active, not passive, involvement and encourage imagination rather than adult control

(Adapted from BC Family Child Care Association 2005)

Toys that work by child power rather than battery power support learning because they require active involvement.

Every time I look through catalogs featuring toys and learning materials, I'm reminded of both the quantity and quality of toys on the market. The number of toys, videos, books, and learning materials to choose from is overwhelming, and manufacturers claim children will learn better and faster when we buy their product. What are we to do? Too often we adults *think* children will like something, so we get it for them. When I did this with my grandchildren, I learned very quickly that the most helpful way to find things that interest them and that they will use is to watch them at play. When we take time to do this, it gives us better insight into how children think and connect with materials.

Toys should suit the age and developmental stage of the child. They should be interesting and inviting; if too easy, the toys become boring; if too hard, they become frustrating. Keep older children's toys separate and out of the reach of younger children as much as possible—older children's toys can present dangers to younger children. The basic guide is the smaller the child, the larger the toy. Anything smaller than a Ping-Pong ball should not be in the hands of children under age three. The key aspect about toy safety is that there are no guarantees a toy is 100 percent safe. Adult supervision is critical to toy safety regardless of the age of the child.

It is nearly impossible to make indestructible toys, but they should be made with durable materials. If you're unsure of the durability of a toy, do your own toy testing by tugging, pulling, and twisting it before allowing the children to use it. Although less expensive toys can save

When imaginative toys like these are set out, hundreds of unique building structures and projects are possible.

you money in the short run, you'll have to replace them more often. This goes for all those great garage sale finds, too, as typically they've had lots of wear and tear before they are sold. Avoid poorly made toys with pieces that can be pulled off and swallowed, such as buttons, wheels, stickers, or labels. Do not buy toys with moving parts that can pinch, scratch, or trap parts of a child's body. If you have toys with strings or cords, keep them shorter than twelve inches to avoid strangulation hazards. Also, toys and materials handled by children should be made from nontoxic materials (surfaces should be lick-able and like-able). The Consumer Product Safety Commission (CPSC) maintains guidelines on acceptable materials for toy manufacturers. Millions of toys have been recalled worldwide due to the use of dangerous

A basket of safe textural materials invites even the youngest children to learn through their senses.

levels of lead or other potential hazards to young children. You can access the complete listing of recalled toys and other items used by or with children on the CPSC website (www.cpsc.gov) and sign up to receive recall updates on children's products (www.recalls.gov).

Choose toys and materials that are open ended and imaginative (can be used in many ways). Such toys help children build self-confidence and use their imaginations. Because there is no right or wrong way to use these toys, children can use them in many creative ways. Ageless open-ended playthings include wooden blocks, Duplo blocks, Lego blocks (but be careful of the small ones, which are choking hazards for young children), puppets, dress-up clothes, and dramatic play accessories.

It's important to have toys that are washable and easily cleaned.

All art and craft materials need to be nontoxic.

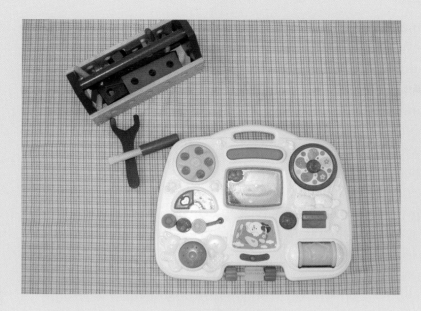

Infants and toddlers enjoy action-reaction toys and experimenting with age-appropriate tools.

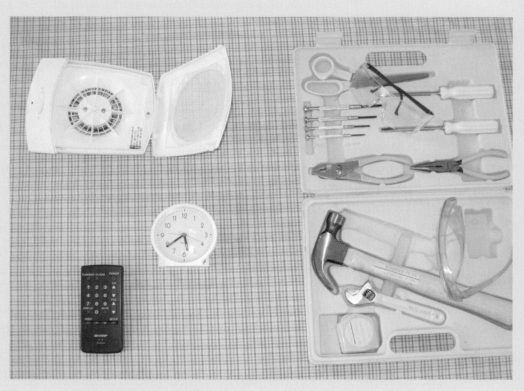

Children can tinker with old but safe mechanical objects (with adult supervision, of course).

Toys should be inviting—colorful and textural (attractive to look at and fun to touch). Many toys for newborns and young infants are constructed with bold, contrasting colors and patterns to encourage them to touch and use the toys. Playthings made of natural materials such as wood, cotton, wicker, and wool are good choices because they have textures that strengthen children's connection with the environment. Even though children may be attracted to the bells and whistles of battery-operated toys, I encourage you to limit the number of this type of toy. Choose toys that run on child power over ones that use battery power. Toys that allow children to use their own power help increase their thinking, reasoning, and logic through discovery and exploration. These are also referred to as action-reaction toys (think of the classic jack-in-the-box).

Cleaning and sanitizing toys and furnishings is critical to keeping children safe and healthy. With recent upsurges in flu and allergies in young children, it is even more important to wash all items thoroughly and often. Look at tags on cloth toys, rugs, and pillows to be sure they are safe to wash and do not need to be dry cleaned. Dry cleaning solvents can be a source of headaches, dizziness, nausea, and eye and skin irritation for children and adults (Kamrin 2001).

With your close supervision, allow older children to examine mechanical pieces such as an old alarm clock or a fan (cut the electrical prongs off the cord to prevent it from being plugged in) or the circuitry in a remote control (remove batteries before giving to the children). Such engaging opportunities help children learn how to think independently and form connections.

In an extensive search of family child care resources, I did not locate any regulatory guidelines or limitations stating the *exact* amount and specific types of materials for children's use. National Association for Family Child Care (NAFCC) standards indicate there should be enough toys and materials to engage children in developmentally appropriate ways (NAFCC 2005). The Family Child Care Environment Rating (FCCER) Scale provides indicators on both the amount and variety of materials based on the age, ability, and number of children enrolled and the type of activity, such as dancing, reading books, or block building.

Furthermore, the FCCER Scale defines "many and varied fine-motor materials" as having a minimum of ten kinds of challenging but not frustrating items for infants and toddlers and a minimum of three kinds of materials for preschool and school-age children in the categories of building toys, manipulatives, art and craft materials, and puzzles. The FCCER also defines "many blocks" as having enough blocks for each age group to keep children from undue competition (Harms, Cryer, and Clifford 2007). In addition to having enough toys within the children's reach, the variety of toys should promote play over a period of time and support total child learning. When deciding what materials and how many to put out, keep in mind the number of children who will want to play with these materials at any one time. The fewer children there are wanting to use a toy at one time, the fewer materials are needed. A regular routine of rotating materials will keep materials exciting as well as provide the variety needed to encourage children to use and learn through them.

Children under age three find "sharing" (sadly often meaning giving away what they have) frustrating, if not impossible. The concept of sharing is not age appropriate for infants and toddlers and should not be an expectation for them. Having enough of their favorite things available to these little ones means you must have at least two of the same types of toys such as two trucks, two dolls, two types of blocks, and so on.

Suggestions for age-appropriate toys and materials follow. This list is meant to help you think about materials that provide children with fun-filled learning experiences. This is a broad spectrum of suggestions, but note that it is not a complete list. What you choose for your program must be based on your goals, your space, and the children in your care.

SUGGESTED MATERIALS FOR LEARNING ZONES

NOTE: These lists should be considered *only* to supplement licensure, accreditation, or other regulatory standards for your FCC program.

Large- and Small-Motor Development for Infants through 24 Months Old (all need to be "tasteable" and washable)

- teethers
- noisemakers—rattles, tambourines, drums, sticks, and bells
- action-reaction toys
- stacking cups
- nested containers
- pop beads
- knob puzzles
- large, lightweight textured balls
- pour-and-carry containers with handles
- lightweight blocks (foam ones not recommended)

- push-and-pull toys
- push walkers (to support early walking feet)
- plastic and soft animals

Large- and Small-Motor Development for Toddlers (18–36 months old)

- variety of balls in varying shapes, sizes, textures
- pop beads and stringing beads over 1 ½ inches in diameter
- knob and simple puzzles (1–5 pieces)
- push-and-pull toys
- toy cars, trucks, airplanes
- stacking cups
- pounding bench and mallet
- nested containers
- things to sort and count
- lacing boards
- toys to ride on (with helmets)
- toys to ride in (with helmets)
- crawl-through tunnel
- pour-and-carry containers with handles
- shapes sorter or ball
- pegboard with large pegs
- parachute
- ribbon wands
- ring toss
- rocking seesaw

Large-Motor Development (preschoolers and up)

- parachute
- balls in varying shapes, sizes, textures
- crawl-through tunnel
- jump rope

- hula hoop
- trike and helmet (protective head gear)
- scooter and helmet
- wagon
- wheelbarrow
- skates and helmet
- beanbags
- hopscotch mat
- exercise mat
- scooter board
- rocking seesaw
- basketball hoop
- balance beam
- balancing board or saucer
- stilts (schoolagers only)
- ring toss
- racing sacks ("potato sacks")
- set of cones
- golf clubs (age-appropriate sizes)
- crawl-through tunnel

NOTE: Materials to support fine-motor skills for children three and up have been included as appropriate in listings for each learning zone that follows.

Arts, Crafts, and Writing Zone

- pencils, colored pencils, pens, erasers, pencil sharpener
- paper such as lined paper, journals, notebooks, cardboard
- markers, both thin and thick
- crayons and chalk
- paints such as fingerpaint, watercolors, tempera
- paint brushes, both thin and thick
- stickers

- stationery

- sponges

- string

- smocks

- paper such as construction, lined, scrap, tissue, newsprint, and old magazines

- fabric and ribbon

- modeling materials like playdough, clay, and modeling tools

- wipe-off board

- chalkboard

- easel

- scissors, both straight and fancy

- hole punchers

- glue and paste

- stapler

- stamps and stamp pads

- ruler

- tape, including clear, colored, and masking

- paper clips and clothespins

- stencils and tracing items

Woodworking Zone

- soft wood (balsa, pine)

- sandpaper

- real tools (small size for small hands)

- nails and screws

- wood glue, string

- tape measure

- safety goggles

- workbench

- apron and tool belt (optional)

Building or Construction Zone

- blocks of all kinds, such as wooden, foam, hollow, and cardboard
- flat wooden boards
- models, such as animals, boats, cars, trucks, and planes
- boxes, both large and small
- plastic containers, including all sizes and nested if possible
- paper rolls, such as from toilet paper, paper towels, and gift wrap
- toothpicks
- wooden dowels
- modeling materials such as playdough, clay, and modeling tools
- Lincoln Logs
- pipe fitters (pipe pieces that twist together)
- Lego blocks
- Tinkertoys
- K'NEX

Dramatic Play Zone

- child-sized table and chairs
- plastic dishes, bowls, cups, and drinking glasses
- placemats
- empty food cartons and tin cans
- toolbox
- housecleaning set
- variety of dolls such as baby dolls (multiracial, gender specific), pretend/play family, dolls with disabilities (with wheelchairs, crutches, and so on)
- dress-up clothes and hats for boys and girls that represent multiple cultures, family types, and careers
- prop boxes
- toy telephones or old (nonworking) cell phones
- toy pots, pans, and cooking and eating utensils
- puppets and puppet stage (optional)
- costumes for performances

Music and Movement Zone

- recorded music from CDs, tapes, and records
- instruments to make music, such as bells, drums, tambourines, rattles, xylophones, and maracas
- almost anything that makes noise
- homemade instruments
- microphone ("real" or toy)
- cassette player and recorder, CD player, or MP3 recorder and player
- books such as song books or picture books with a music theme
- scarves and ribbon streamers

Quiet or Relaxing Zone

- puzzles
- beads such as pop beads (infants–toddlers) and stringing beads (preschoolers and up)
- container of tactile materials such as beanbags, Koosh ball, nylon net ball, large seashells, or smooth rocks (at least 1 ½ inches in diameter)
- photo album of the children, their families, and people they know
- pillows, comfortable rug, or chair
- books to read or look at
- plants
- materials for journaling, including pencils and paper
- plants

Friendship Zone

- large area rug
- pillows
- open space to create in, hang out with friends, and move or groove

Literacy Zone (works well as a homework zone for schoolagers)

- comfortable space to read
- comfortable space for homework (schoolagers)
- scrapbook of your special FCC activities
- photo albums of children and families
- homemade books
- crossword puzzles and word searches (schoolagers)
- homework toolkit—ruler, pencils, erasers, calculator, and so on
- variety of reading material
    - storybooks for each age group of children: cloth or board books, picture books, and early readers (include chapter books if you have advanced readers)
    - reference and nonfiction books such as children's dictionaries, word books, encyclopedias, and books about science, nature, discovery, and geography
    - children's magazines

Science or Discovery Zone

- magnifying glass (unbreakable) and hand-held microscope
- small mirrors (unbreakable)
- thermometer (unbreakable and easy to read)
- eye droppers
- hourglass, timer, and working clock
- prisms (unbreakable)
- color paddles
- kaleidoscopes
- magnets (at least 1 ½ inches in diameter)
- simple, easy-to-read maps of your city or state (and beyond for schoolagers)
- flashlights
- small plastic bottles and tubes
- compass
- plastic animals
- binoculars

Nature Zone

- terrarium
- pet with protective cage, aquarium, or fish bowl with fish and plants
- bug catcher
- ant farm
- materials for growing plants, such as seeds, dirt, unbreakable pots, watering can, and gardening tools
- seashells
- smooth rocks at least 1 ½ inches in diameter
- pinecones, seeds
- twigs, branches, bark, and cut pieces of tree limbs or trunk
- variety of preserved leaves (in scrapbook or notebook or laminated)
- variety of plastic animals, such as pets, farm, zoo, water, and birds

Math Zone

- counters
- pop beads or stringing beads
- stacking rings of varying sizes and nesting containers
- linking or fit-together cubes
- parquet or pattern blocks (with cards recommended for schoolagers)
- solid shapes set (for example, cylinder, ball, or cube)
- dominoes
- calculator
- abacus
- ruler, yardstick, and tape measure
- nonstandard measuring tools such as string, dowels, or thin wooden poles
- balancing scale and weights
- dice
- deck of playing cards (number cards only)
- graph paper or mat
- play money and cash register

Texture or Sensory Zone

- large containers (for example, plastic storage container or baby bathtub) or sand/water table
- cups, pitcher, funnel, and sifter
- eye droppers
- squeeze or spray bottles
- spoons
- sponges
- thin, clear plastic tubes or hoses
- buckets
- boats
- sand shovel
- sand molds
- seashells
- waterproof aprons or smocks
- mops and buckets to help clean up after playing

For ages three and up

- wood chips (those used for pet cages and barbecue grills have wonderful smells)
- seeds
- feathers
- bark
- beads
- buttons
- paper confetti
- artificial flowers (blossoms only)

NOTE: Uncooked food items such as macaroni, oatmeal, and rice are NOT recommended as playthings for children of any age.

○ ○ ○

This chapter has suggested elements needed to extend the feeling of your home into your child care space. Recommendations have been given for creating a homestyle environment that is supportive of all children's learning experiences. There are no set guidelines or regulations for designing your child care space—it's not a "one size fits all" concept. Rather, you must decide what feeling you want to promote based on your goals for the children and the space in your home.

These rooms use homelike furnishings to bring together business and residence in a comfortable way.

Chapter 5 discusses how to connect children with nature through an exciting outdoor learning environment. It offers suggestions to create or redesign your outdoor space, including diagrams and photos of outdoor environments that go beyond playground equipment.

Activities and Questions

A well-designed and functional environment is one that welcomes children to play and stay. Take this book into your child care space, sit on the floor or on a short chair, and answer the following questions. To get the best perspective and answers, do this while the children are busy in the environment.

1   Does your entryway welcome children, families, and visitors? Do cubbies take up a large amount of space? What alternatives could you use for the children's belongings while still providing ready access to their personal things?

2   Does the furniture take up more than half the room? How can you consolidate interest centers into zones such as those mentioned in this chapter?

3   Does the style of furniture and the atmosphere in the child care space feel like home or is it noticeably different? How can you create a more homelike feeling that is comfortable and cozy as well as supportive of children's learning needs?

4   Watch the children as they play. What are the most popular areas? Least used areas? How can you create an environment (such as by rotating, removing, or redesigning the play spaces) that invites them to explore and learn in all areas?

5   Considering the ages of the children, their skills, and your goals for them, does your present child care arrangement promote exciting learning experiences? What parts are you satisfied with? Dissatisfied with? What changes can you make to the environment to help children become independent learners?

6   Do all the children want to do everything at the same time? How can you arrange the environment (such as activities, materials, and the daily schedule) to encourage children to move freely from one activity to another or one place to another?

5

Creating a Rich and Complex Outdoor Environment

Children and the great outdoors are a perfect match. When they are outside, they have our permission to run, climb, scream, and jump around until they drop. All of this is in the name of fun—or is it?

When children appear bored, disinterested, "hyper," or challenging, one of my first thoughts is to open the door and take them outside. Children have a special connection with the outdoors. Because the value of outdoor play is so important, you need to look carefully at your backyard outdoor environment. Does it invite and support children's play, fitness, and discovery? A lot of learning can take place in outdoor environments that support exploration and creativity as well as physical exercise.

When I was a kindergarten teacher, I chose to do most of my observations on the playground. I could tell more about children while they were outside than anywhere else. Their play involved risk

Come outside with me today

Take my hand

We will play

We will learn and nature teach

All her wonders are within our reach

—PETER STEWART

taking (going down the big slide), decision making (which friend to play with), thinking skills (wondering what might happen to them if they threw a ball into a filled water table), and cooperation (no one can be the team leader every day). They practiced skills in all learning domains, from getting a ball through the basketball hoop (large motor) to forming a sand castle with a twig flag on top (fine motor and creativity). And outside I saw children concentrating for longer periods of time than when they were inside.

We all need sunlight and fresh air for healthy bodies. Medical experts indicate children especially need some time outdoors every day to ward off disease and keep them connected with nature. Environmentalists and others who care about the future of our planet understand that children have to love the earth before they can save it.

A safe but exciting backyard environment is not optional; rather, it's a vital part of a homestyle FCC program and an extension of your indoor learning environment. When you create a rich and complex outdoor environment geared for children's ages, abilities, and development, you are well on your way to connecting children with nature. This chapter gives you some ideas to think through as you evaluate and redesign or plan the outdoor space available to the children in your care.

This child plays outdoors and explores nature in the safety of the FCC program's backyard.

These providers know the importance
of close supervision during active and
challenging outdoor play.

Outdoor Play Areas

Your outdoor environment should be made up of safe places that are challenging but not hazardous. A *challenge* is what children see, but a *hazard* is often a factor not apparent to them (Ferguson 1986). There are no guarantees that a place, activity, or toy is completely safe. In fact, the U.S. Consumer Product Safety Commission (CPSC) estimates that 80 percent of injuries on playgrounds involve children falling from play equipment. Other injuries happen when children are hit by swings or other moving equipment, or get entangled in ropes or cords attached to play equipment (CPSC 2005). With good planning and close supervision, outdoor environments stretch children's muscles and their learning. Thus it is your job to identify and correct potential problem areas, toys, or equipment.

Maintain outdoor materials in the same way you keep your indoor materials safe and clean. A safety checklist from the CPSC *Outdoor Home Playground Safety Handbook* is reprinted in this book as appendix F. The checklist offers a condensed but thorough list of tips and reminders about setting up and maintaining outdoor play equipment. Although following the standards in the CPSC handbook is not mandatory, it is highly recommended.

Challenging play does not refer to children moving from place to place without regard for their safety or that of others. A designed play area can lead to creative and challenging play while also helping to ensure safety. You need to supervise closely and observe whether the children are interacting with the outside environment in unexpected ways that may not be safe.

To create an outdoor play place for children that is both safe and challenging, first consider locating it where the children will be visible to you at all times. This may mean removing plastic shutters from a playhouse or lower limbs from a shade tree. It also means that play structures made of metal must be located in areas protected from the sun. Keep infants and toddlers safe in a smaller secured space just for them. Use small bushes to create a natural fence between the busier play area and the area where the infants and toddlers typically play—you can see over it and the children can easily move between areas if they want to. Remember, close supervision is critical to the safe play of children.

This quaint playhouse acts as a canvas for safe, expressive outdoor play. The window shutters have been removed to provide better line-of-sight supervision while the children are inside the playhouse.

Children of all ages need opportunities to take risks and test their skills. Trial and error results in more cautious behavior and safer play. Outdoor play structures come in all sizes, price ranges, and materials. Challenging and safe play structures (playground equipment) should have the following features:

- durable construction from materials appropriate for your climate

- poles buried and anchored in concrete

- handrails and large platform areas

- openings larger than the smallest child's head

- no sharp edges, exposed long bolts, "s" hooks, or splintering wood

- a minimum of two different ways to enter and exit (rope ladder, step ladder, sliding pole, and so on)

- varying complexity and safe features for use by children of all ages (check manufacturer's age recommendations to ensure children's safety)

- adequate fall zone under and around all climbing equipment and swings (play structures where children climb or play above ground level must be separated by a minimum of six feet)

- play choices such as active, quiet, alone, with friends, uninvolved (just watching), or eating outside

- play possibilities that encourage children's imaginative, creative play (for example, a playhouse or a small boat or car)

- enclosed or semi-enclosed space (that still allows you to supervise closely)

- play space in the lower part of a climber, such as a movable plastic table for tea parties, a small bench, a basket of books for reading, or an easel for painting a landscape masterpiece

Most playgrounds have commercial equipment, but you need not feel required to purchase it. Materials such as graduated tree trunks, cable spools, scrap pipe, and barrels can be used to build challenging play structures for children ages three and up (Isenberg and Quisenberry 2002). When using materials not intended for a playground use, it is absolutely critical to ensure that all materials are nontoxic and that they follow the safety guidelines for playground equipment found in appendix F. Children should be allowed to use the equipment under constant supervision only after all surfaces have been smoothed until nearly polished and all loose parts have been removed.

These outdoor play structures made with quality construction materials are built to last and to ensure children's safety.

These guardrails with open slats both protect children from falling and assist the provider in supervising children as they play.

This sunny and semi-enclosed space under the climbing structure invites children to enjoy quiet play.

These play
structures
inspire creative
play and
help children
explore their
imaginations.

Natural Play Yards

A backyard environment that children love and learn from is more than play structures and toys—it also includes opportunities for children to connect to nature and natural elements. An outdoor environment goal should be to preserve the natural state where children can find something new everywhere they play. Elements to connect children with nature can include the following:

- variety of terrain, for example, ditches, slopes, or dirt mounds for climbing, hiding, rolling, sliding, or just sitting to enjoy little creatures living there
- varying ground cover, for example, grass, sand, wood chips, pebbles, or mulch (NOTE: keep safety and choking hazards in mind as you choose surfacing materials)
- garden to grow good things to eat, attract butterflies, birds, and bugs, or enjoy the fragrance of the flowers
- well-protected or well-supervised water feature, for example, a small pond, stream, sprinklers, or water table
- area for animals and housing for them
- stepping stones (children can make these from concrete and small pebbles molded in large garden pots or plastic drip pans)
- wishing well
- areas for digging, building sand castles, or constructing roads or dams
- trees safe to climb (you may want to allow this only for short periods of closely supervised playtime)
- hideouts (playhouse, tent, low-limb tree house, natural hideout in a shrub or tree, trellis frame, flowering vine, blankets or cloths tossed over a box or table)
- wind chimes and bells (not too loud or you may hear from your neighbors)
- greenhouse or enclosed growing shed
- gathering or resting area

Note that swimming pools are not included in this list; pools must be fenced with a lockable gate while children are in your care. Even very small ponds, such as where water accumulates under a water feature or a tiny pond with fish, represent a drowning hazard as much as a deeper wading pool or swimming pool. If you have a permanent water feature, consider installing a grate one inch below the surface to prevent children from falling in or drowning.

By mixing in the beauty of nature, this outdoor
exploration area and the ones on the following
pages encourage children to interact with the
world around them.

This provider has installed fencing across the
entire swimming pool area to protect children
while they are enjoying an outdoor picnic.

Outdoor Design

Children need visual cues and simple names to help them make sense of the environment and play safely. Just as you have designed boundaries for your indoor environment, it is equally important to have clear definition outside. As you design your outdoor environment, be sure to have enough room for children to move freely without getting into each other's way and room for play opportunities for children of differing abilities and ages. The outdoor illustration below offers outdoor play area suggestions. By creating well-defined areas, the children can move freely and have many opportunities to explore and enjoy the great outdoors.

This carefully designed outdoor plan connects children with nature and provides opportunities for active and passive play.

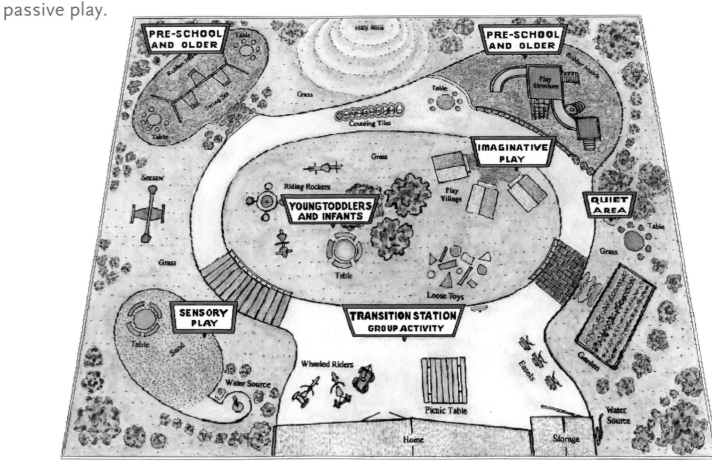

Here are some suggestions for creating well-defined outdoor places and spaces:

- transition station—a small but open area inside or just outside the door that allows children to look around before deciding where they will play

- small, safe, and secured space for infants and young toddlers

- lots of open pathways around play structures, or to the garden, or for moving from area to area using wheeled toys, or for a wheelchair (If you care for a child in a wheelchair or a child with limited mobility, construct solid-surface pathways with materials such as concrete, asphalt, or rubberized fall-zone material.)

- area for sensory play such as a sandbox, water table, or with twigs, leaves, dirt, gravel, or wood chips

- areas for imaginative play such as a playhouse, large boat, toy vehicles, toy animals, dress-up clothes (weather permitting)

- picnic or patio table for items brought outside, for picnics, cooking or art projects, or just to sit and talk

- hard-surfaced areas for games, dancing, and other group activities

- quiet, soft place to relax, daydream, watch the clouds, read a book

- hideout away from active play areas

- areas for a variety of active play choices: for riding, swinging, climbing, playing games, digging

- open grassy areas for moving freely, or to perform in a play or have a picnic

- large storage to hold tools, toys, or items not for child care use

- varying terrain and ground cover: small hills, ramps, grass, sand, mulch, hard surfaces

- raised beds or containers for growing edible plants

- outdoor animal care area

- color-coded play structures or activities coded according to complexity, for example, green = safe for all children's use, yellow = safe for preschoolers and up, red = safe for schoolagers only

A transition space allows children to move gradually from inside to outside. It is also a convenient spot for putting on or removing clothing for active outdoor play.

When not in use, sandboxes and sand tables—regardless of size—must be covered to keep sand clean.

Materials can be stored and taken outdoors to any location—even to the beach or on a nature walk.

These are areas where children can enjoy nature and each other's company.

A well-arranged backyard environment facilitates children's play and allows them to move easily from place to place.

Different methods of labeling and organizing this outdoor cabinet help the provider locate materials easily.

Having outdoor rules ensures safe play for children of all ages and abilities. Posting your rules and reviewing them often reminds the children of their importance.

Creating an Accessible Outdoor Environment for Children with Special Needs

Although many changes or modifications have been made to the insides of facilities, traditional playground equipment and design continue to present problems for children with special needs. As a special education teacher, I often saw children with special needs sitting by themselves watching their friends play. In all kinds of ways, a well-planned and safe outdoor environment ensures that outdoor play is equally accessible for all children.

The goals in creating a playground appropriate for children with special needs are twofold: children with special needs should be as involved in play as typically developing children are, and equipment and play structures must allow them to develop physical and social skills.

The term *accessibility* means "the equipment is both easy to get to and, once on the equipment, is easy for a child to play on independently and safely" (Davis 2005, 20). In play environments, accessibility can mean children with special needs should have access to a variety (not all) of the play opportunities just as typically developing children do. I have so far been unable to determine whether accessibility guidelines for playgrounds are a part of federal mandates.

Hard surfaces on sidewalks and pathways allow children with disabilities easy access to outdoor play activities.

This ramp allows children to ride wheeled vehicles and is also wide enough for wheelchair access.

A diagnosis of having special needs pertains to children's disabilities not their capabilities. A well-designed outdoor environment supports the part of a child with special needs that is healthy and capable. As you plan or make adaptations for children with disabilities, consider what they *can* do (their abilities). This will help engage them and will certainly support their self-confidence as well as their development. When planning an accessible outdoor environment, do not isolate or separate accessible spaces from the rest of the play areas. Consider using brightly colored equipment or color cues to help children with special needs locate the areas and equipment that are safe for them to use. Also consider using the ground cover or texture on the playground to indicate pathways and areas where adaptive play equipment is located. Solid surface pathways and benches should be available for children who use wheelchairs or crutches. Install guardrails leading to and from equipment to help ensure safety and promote the child's feeling of "I can do it." When provided with accessible and safe play equipment, children with special needs engage in play in the same manner as typically developing children do.

○ ○ ○

The great outdoors is a place that provides another dimension to children's learning. For young children, spending time outside is more than just playing on playground equipment—it also means connecting with nature. If you do not have natural play spaces, start small by using what you have on hand and expand slowly to create spots where children can explore, discover, and get connected with the outdoor world. Simple adaptations and modifications to outside play areas provide opportunities for children with special needs to be involved in activities and move freely, much as their typically developing peers do.

These children are experiencing a new snowfall and exploring winter's wonders.

Activities and Questions

Well-designed outdoor environments should be fun and safe places for children to get connected with nature, places that encourage active play and expand indoor learning experiences. Ask yourself the following questions as you design, change, and enrich your outdoor play spaces:

1   Look at the area just inside and outside the door used to access your outdoor play area. Do children have a breathing space between being inside and stepping out into the outdoor play space? If not, how can you create a small transition area?

2   Are there places in the outdoor environment where children can rest, relax, or enjoy passive play activities such as bird or cloud watching, reading a book, or simply watching friends at play?

3   Take your shoes off and go barefoot in your outdoor environment. Do you feel at least three different ground cover textures? Do these ground covers support the children's connection to nature? What simple changes could or should be made?

4   Besides playground equipment and wheeled toys, what other outdoor play options are there? Are children connected to nature as they play?

5   What types of living things do children care for in the outdoor environment? Pets? Plants? A garden? Small critters such as birds, ladybugs, worms, or butterflies?

6   If you enrolled a child with special needs tomorrow, would there be some accessibility to outdoor play for him?

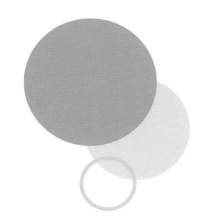

Conclusion: Home Sweet FCC Home

If you have made it to these last few pages and are still reading, you probably want to know how the book ends—but this is one story that never does. The process of creating comfortable learning places where children thrive is never-ending. Just like the little bunny who continues to work on long-lasting batteries in television commercials, you will keep planning, designing, and creating places and spaces for your FCC program—not as a decorator but as an educator.

The goal of this book is to inspire you to create learning environments that nurture the warm and caring feeling of home. I hope you have felt encouraged and freed to remove institutional elements and extend your home into your child care space. Except for having floors, ceilings, and four walls, homes are not like other learning institutions and they shouldn't look like those places. There is no one way to create a homestyle environment, but the critical elements necessary for supporting children's learning experiences have been discussed and documented with photography throughout

A loving atmosphere in your home is the foundation for your life.

—TENZIN GYATSO,
14TH DALAI LAMA

this book. I hope what you've read has given you many ideas. If you have photos and suggestions of your own, I would love to hear from you. I can be reached by email at consultljarmstrong@yahoo.com.

Here is one last look at the top ten ways we've explored for creating exciting homestyle places for children's learning and spaces that also are a great addition to your home.

1   Start with a goal, then develop your ideas. What is it that you want for the children in your program, your own family, yourself?

2   Create a blank slate by stripping the environment mentally (or physically if you are currently licensed and have already set up your child care spaces).

3   Watch the children to see how your environment supports their learning. Watch their behavior and interactions to determine whether everything's working smoothly. Do you need to make adjustments?

4   Remove the clutter—less clutter creates more places for learning spaces.

5   Sort, clean, remove materials, and even paint (ideally with the children's assistance) over a period of time. Young children need a predictable environment to maintain their sense of security and competence.

6   Deinstitutionalize the environment: rebuild carefully, using natural materials, soft tones or neutral colors, a well-thought-out room arrangement, and wall displays that are meaningful to the children.

7   Look at your child care space. Does it communicate a sense of comfort, beauty, and calm?

8   Ask yourself, Is this a place where children love to be, love to learn, and love to stay? Is this a place where I like to be, one that doesn't intrude on my own family, yet keeps the feeling of my home?

9   Look at the environment from a child's perspective. Move around on your knees to see how children feel when they're in this place. Keep in mind that children's basic needs must be met before they can learn.

10 Never stop dreaming and creating and recreating your family child care environment as a great place for children to wander and wonder. And remember, there's no one right way—just your way.

Appendix A:
For New Providers

Opening a home-based family child care (FCC) business often involves an unexpected metamorphosis for your home and your family. Remember that first, last, and always your home is where your family resides—providing family child care in your home should not push your family's needs aside. The more accepting your family is about sharing their living space with your business, the happier your home will be at all hours every day. Your home meets your family's needs in these ways:

- It's a place where your family shares their joys, problems, and laughter, and where memories are made over the years.

- It's a safe place to relax and retreat from the hectic pace that we all experience.

- It's both comfortable and personal, and it reflects family members' personalities, family background, and all that's important to your family.

Designing a family child care environment in your home that also accommodates the needs of your family involves a business partnership between you and your family members. All too often, family members are not consulted about this new venture and look on in amazement as the feeling of home is replaced with institutional tables and chairs, filing cabinets, bulletin boards, metal furniture, and perhaps even a rug telling them how to say hello in ten languages.

Include your family as your advisers or your board of directors to help you decide the location of your child care space, their involvement (if any) during hours of operation, and yes, maybe even their involvement as investors. "Sweat equity" or the sharing of toys, books, or even allowance money can be part of their partnership in the business, with the promise of a great return on their investment. Recently, I visited a provider whose oldest daughter was her assistant. Her husband had renovated their basement for child care. They had developed a business charter that was signed by all family members, and dividends were given out quarterly.

Designing exciting environments for children is much like following a prize-winning recipe: start with a table and chairs for all the children; add blocks, puzzles, and art materials; use a pinch of color and lots of light.

Mix together and let stand for a few days until used. Serves the exact number of children in your family child care program.

Creating an Environment That Meets the Needs of Your Family

Once you've made your decision to open your home to care for children, it's equally important that family members living in the house buy into this venture. As you determine which area(s) of the house will be used for child care, include family members in this decision—especially your own children. After all, they will need to share not only a parent but often their toys, books, pets, backyard playhouse, and perhaps even their family room with other children. Spouses will want to have a say about where their favorite chair will be relocated, the use of their recreational items, or where media equipment can be put to keep it safe from inquisitive minds and fingers.

Discuss what your goals for FCC services are, the number of children you will ideally have, your hours of operation, and which areas of the house and yard you will use. Since your family members will be spending the most time in the house, their needs must be considered first as you work to create balance between your business and your family! Asking for their help with plans and decisions gives them a voice and a partnership role in your family child care program. A good way to encourage that partnership is to decide together which spaces within your home to keep for your family and not use for child care. You can accomplish this by asking your own questions and encouraging your family members to ask their questions:

- Where do you and your family spend most of your time together?
- What furniture, books, wall hangings, and so on are important to keep intact?
- Are there locations in your front or back yard that should not be used by the children?
- Which door do you most often use as you enter or leave your house?
- Which phone would best be used for family calls, and which one should be used for child care calls?

- What are family members' concerns about issues such as the spaces they need and want, and privacy?

- How accepting are they about some areas being off-limits during child care hours?

- Can family members use the child care space when the child care business is not open?

- How will family members know which food items are meant for the child care children and what is available for family members looking for a snack or a meal?

- Can family members expect any financial compensation from the child care business?

- Who is responsible for cleaning the child care space indoors and outdoors?

- Will the family home still look the same?

- Will there be lots of changes in places where family members like to hang out? What happens to the pets?

This child snuggles up to the family's dog at a family child care home.

A good way to be sure family needs are met is to establish ground rules that all family members can agree on. Once agreement has been reached, write down the ground rules so all family members can refer to them from time to time, or when issues must be renegotiated. An example of what these written rules might look like follows.

Date: _April 28_

We have agreed to accommodate child care in our home following these
ground rules:

1   Family room and outside play area will be off-limits to family during child
    care hours.

2   Living room, dining room, bedrooms, front yard, and garage will be off-limits
    to children in care.

3   Kitchen space should not be used during child care hours due to health and
    food-handling regulations. (Check your licensure policies for clarification.)

4   Phone calls will be handled by a separate phone line, a designated cell phone
    number, or a voice mail system on the home phone.

5   The space designated as office space will have child care business–related
    information kept in a locked cabinet; this space will be off-limits to family
    members.

6   Family items such as media equipment, toys, books, or clothing will not be
    used for the child care program unless previously agreed upon by family
    members.

7   No business-based activities will take place in the home during times when
    the child care program is closed.

Signed by:

Getting Organized

As you plan and design your child care environment, you will accumulate information you need to consider before the first child walks through your door. Since organization is essential for a busy family child care provider, begin by purchasing a sturdy container, an expandable file with multiple pockets, or another type of filing system. It will help you organize both the requirements and the resources needed for your family child care program.

Although many websites and resources offer help in giving direction to your program, the source of no-cost information I have found most helpful is the National Resource Center for Health and Safety in Child Care and Early Education (NRC) (1-800-598-KIDS; www.nrckids.org). Two of their no-cost resources that will help you most are available on the NRC website:

- State Licensing and Regulation Information tab: Click on the state where you'll be operating your program and find the family child care guidelines for that state. You can download these for your files and planning.

- Building Blocks: A downloadable tool to help provide child care professionals with quality standards and guidelines. Located under the For Child Care Providers tab.

The National Association of Child Care Resource and Referral Agencies (www.naccrra.org) provides the definition of family child care as determined by each state. The website also has information on child care licensing requirements, including minimum early childhood education (ECE) preservice qualifications, orientation/initial licensure, and annual ongoing training hours for family child care providers.

The National Association for Family Child Care (NAFCC) (1-800-359-3817; http://nafcc.net) is another great source of information. NAFCC is a nonprofit organization dedicated to the support and accreditation of family child care. Its mission is to strengthen the profession of family child care through professional development and leadership.

You will undoubtedly come across many more sources of information, so please view these as just places to start your resource file.

The next step is to look for an ideal location for your program. Consider two things: understanding health and safety guidelines, and setting goals for the children and your program. Both will provide a useful framework for finding the best spot in your home to meet child care needs. These topics are addressed in appendixes B and C.

Choosing the right location for a family
child care business can be challenging,
but imagining the potential of blank spaces
like these can be fun and rewarding.

Appendix B:
Health and Safety Guidelines

Did you know that a recent study asking low-income parents why they selected their family child care provider indicated safety was one of the most important reasons (Layzer, Goodson, and Brown-Lyons 2007)? Regardless of income, families trust you with the most precious thing they have—their child. Keeping children protected from harm in your home is both a privilege and a huge responsibility. The look of a "safe" child care environment is one having a reduced potential for hazards through careful selection of toys, furnishings, materials, and supplies, and the constant supervision of children. Although you cannot ensure 100 percent safety and health for the children, you can do many things to keep them safe and healthy.

As a child care provider, what you do or don't do impacts the lives of the children in your care and your own family members. Many providers can testify to having saved the lives of children in their care because they paid close attention to safety codes, had completed safety checklists, and practiced home evacuations regularly. As with your car and home liability insurance policies, nothing is needed until an emergency arises.

Know the Rules

Creating and maintaining a safe and healthy environment is the most important consideration in quality family child care. Such an environment helps children move safely and easily from place to place and gives you peace of mind through knowing you have identified and eliminated potential hazards. In most states, family child care providers are expected to comply with standards and guidelines for licensure, including applicable requirements for safety, health, and fire prevention. You should consider licensure standards your primary source of guidance if you live in a state with FCC regulations. In addition, the list at the top of page 186 includes my own key reminders to keep your family and the children in your care healthy and protected from harm.

By using safety gates, this provider keeps children safely away from a potentially harmful kitchen.

- Become familiar with fire and building codes and licensure safety standards from your local fire department or licensing agency, especially those standards regulating the use of open flame (such as candles, fireplaces, and kerosene heaters) during hours of operation.

- Check fabrics, upholstery materials, and carpets for flammable materials.

- Keep wall and hanging displays to a minimum. (The National Life Safety Code indicates 80 percent or more of wall space should be free of paper or other flammable materials.)

- Check rug and carpet cleaning solvents. (These are a potential source of poisoning, especially for infants and children playing on the rugs or carpeting.)

- If you need to use pesticides indoors or outside, use baits in self-contained, tamper-resistant stations or gels in cracks and crevices that are out of the reach and sight of children.

- Invest in a quality and user-friendly home security system.

- Purchase a battery-operated or hand-cracked weather monitor and flashlight and keep them functioning.

- Purchase at least one extra battery for your cell phone and keep it charged.

Use the Rules

Creating and maintaining an environment with a focus on personal safety and well-being is not an option, it is a responsibility. You must provide a setting that is safe and sanitary. Keeping children safe requires awareness of potentially hazardous areas and regular safety procedures and home inspections. Helping children stay healthy requires keeping everyone and everything clean. As mentioned before, licensure standards must guide your health and safety practices. Consider the list below a supplement to all regulatory guidelines for your program.

- Keep clear a minimum of two pathways (exits) out of your child care space and home.

- Conduct fire evacuations monthly.

- Keep a kit packed with everything you and the children might need in case of an emergency or evacuation.

- Install smoke detectors and carbon monoxide detectors, and test them monthly to ensure they are functioning properly.

- Keep fire extinguishers in good working order in easy access locations near open flames and in the kitchen.

- Keep electrical outlets covered and extension cords out of children's reach.

- Conduct regular safety checks in all indoor and outdoor areas.

- Have water tested regularly for purity and mineral content, especially if you use well water.

Additional safety hazards identified recently have focused on recalls of toys and children's furniture. High percentages of toys and furniture manufactured in countries that lack the strict U.S. inspection and quality assurance procedures are recalled due to lead-based paint on toys and poor construction of furniture. To monitor the safety of such products, check the U.S. Consumer Product Safety Commission's website (www.recalls.gov) and sign up to receive notifications for all children's product recalls. This is a fast, no-cost way to keep your entire home a safe place.

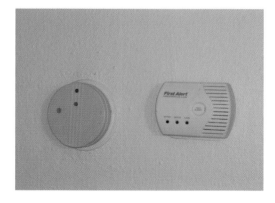

Functioning fire extinguishers, smoke detectors, and carbon monoxide detectors boost safety and are typically required in spaces where child care is conducted.

A Healthy Environment

What do parents look for in a family child care environment? They want an environment that looks and smells clean. Your licensing standards outline sanitation requirements and procedures—but the bottom line is that toys, floors, walls, the kitchen, your hands, and the children must be kept sparkling clean. This doesn't mean children shouldn't dig in the backyard or get dirty playing with wet sand! It does mean that when the fun is over, the children and the space should be cleaned. Remember to wash your hands and have the children wash their hands often, and remember to sanitize the changing table area after every diaper change. If your home is poorly kept, families won't want to enroll their children in your program.

The term *environmental health* refers to elements that affect the health of humans, both negatively and positively. Children's developing immune systems and growing brains make them especially susceptible to environmental hazards. For a complete review of environmental health, use the *Go Green Rating Scale for Early Childhood Settings* (Boise 2010). Exposure to lead and exposure to indoor air contaminants are two common, yet easily addressed environmental hazards in homes. If you have plumbing that was installed before 1987, you need to check for lead.

Water pipes made of lead, copper, and even some plastics may contribute to drinking water contamination. Lead can leach into drinking water from certain types of plumbing materials (lead pipes, copper pipes with lead solder, and brass faucets). Although water is not usually a primary source of children's exposure to lead, formula-fed infants are at risk of lead poisoning if their formula is made with lead-contaminated water. In some neighborhoods and rural communities, lead pipes buried underground contaminate water entering the house and possibly even the soil around the pipes. Test water coming out of the tap you use for drinking water to ensure it is lead-free and/or use a filter that traps lead particles.

Lead-based paint used in older homes is by far the most common source of lead poisoning. If your home was built prior to 1978, it may be among the 38 million houses that potentially could contain lead-based paint either inside or on the exterior. Lead-based paint that is not peeling or flaking off does not pose an immediate concern, but children who chew paint chips or even suck on their hands have exposed themselves to lead dust. Investing in a lead-based paint analysis is money well spent (U.S. Environmental Protection Agency 2003).

A healthy environment with good indoor air quality is extremely important. Unhealthy air is a threat to children's respiratory health. The number of children who suffer from allergies and asthma increases every year. It is

These bathrooms' fun and whimsical designs help make washing hands fun.

such a problem that the U.S. Environmental Protection Agency (2008) lists poor indoor air quality as a major environmental health concern.

You can improve indoor air by lowering the amount of toxins you use and by bringing fresh air in from outside. Outdoor air dilutes or carries away emissions from pollutants. Typically, air enters and leaves your home through open windows and doors, although weather conditions sometimes don't allow these pathways to be kept wide open. Opening a window just slightly from the top (to keep drafts off children), leaving an exhaust fan on in the kitchen or bathroom, or setting your thermostat to automatic fan can help keep the air moving, pollutant levels down, and your home smelling fresh.

Asbestos-containing materials are very common in homes built or remodeled before the 1970s. Asbestos is a health hazard when it crumbles and releases particles into the air. Fortunately, most individuals exposed to small amounts of asbestos do not develop asbestos-related health problems. There is, however, no known safe level of exposure, so all exposure to asbestos should be avoided. As with lead-based paint removal, having an expert remove asbestos in your home is very important (U.S. Environmental Protection Agency 2010).

Look for these potential pollutant sources in your home:

- heating and cooling systems
- open flames; for example, stoves, furnaces, fireplaces, space heaters
- humidifiers and air vaporizers
- wet or damp carpets or rugs, which can be sources of mold and mildew
- combustion sources such as oil, gas, kerosene, wood, tobacco products, cleaning solvents
- radon
- asbestos
- pets with feathers, fur, or hair
- overspray or residue of pesticides used inside or outdoors
- dust
- cockroaches
- products that emit an odor while drying (such as paint)
- products made using formaldehyde
- vehicle exhaust that enters the house
- candles and air fresheners

(Boise 2010)

Here are some suggestions to reduce airborne pollutants and germs:

- Choose washable rather than dry-clean-only upholstery and window fabrics.
- Reduce the amount of carpeting and increase use of hardwood or other resilient floors such as tile.
- Clean air ducts regularly.
- Replace furnace or air conditioning unit filters regularly. (Some sources suggest changing filters every month if the unit is used daily.)
- Vacuum at least three times weekly.
- Steam clean or wash rugs, carpets, floors, and outdoor play equipment after all pesticide treatments.

Here are ways to keep your child care environment clean and healthy:

- Clean all washable toys in your dishwasher using a mild bleach solution. Rinse toys in water to remove bleach residue. Air drying is highly recommended.
- Clean spills on your rugs and carpets with a brush and hot water. This will bring up most spots without leaving a residue like carpet cleaning solvents do. (For stubborn stains sometimes I add a small amount of dishwashing detergent to the water.)
- To keep wicker baskets clean and dust-free, spray them with a mild bleach solution and dry them in the sun.
- Remember that washed items dried in the sun are actually cleaner than those dried in a dryer. The sun helps to kill bacteria (and they smell fresh too).
- Use a hair dryer on medium heat to get crayon marks off walls, floors, and even wallpaper. Wipe with a damp cloth and a little cleaning liquid.

(www.housecleaning-tips.com)

In conclusion, use the Scouting motto, "Be Prepared." Be alert and observant for potentially harmful or unsafe conditions. Listen to families' concerns or suggestions to keep their children safe and healthy. Clean all surfaces and materials within reach of children often. Ask a neighbor you trust to be "on call" to assist in an emergency or to provide a place of respite or safety. Make keeping your child care environment smelling and looking clean a daily priority. As a result, everyone spending time in your home will be safer and healthier.

Appendix C: Setting Goals for the Children and Your Program

When you start out on a journey, you usually want to know where you're going and how to get there. Without a map (or now a GPS), you would simply be guessing which way to go or where to turn. It's the same for your child care program—it helps to have a destination and a plan. Your program goals and your goals for individual children represent your destination. Your plan describes how you'll achieve your goals. What is it you want the children in your care to experience, learn, and keep with them as memories of being in your care? Setting up goals for your program and the children depends on many things:

- age of the children
- interests of the children
- special needs of the children, including disabilities or giftedness
- amount of time spent in your program

Setting goals for each child is helpful as you set up your environment and plan learning experiences. Goal setting is a process you should use initially and then revisit periodically to see whether you need to make adjustments as your group of children changes. Dennis Vicars (2010) developed five indicators of quality learning places for young children using the acronym "SCOPE": Safe, Clean, Organized, Professional, and Educational. When you begin writing your goals remember SCOPE.

Once you have set your goals, keep your list in a place where you can refer to it often. Better yet, create a scrapbook or a photo album showcasing your goals and display it in a prominent place where families and visitors can look at it. You may even find it helpful to have families' input as you set goals for their children. Knowing the children and establishing learning memories for them is an important first step in designing your environment.

This provider's scrapbook shows her professional commitment and showcases children's learning activities.

Appendix D: Staging and Arranging Grid

Appendix E:
Materials Inventory

Age of Children	Materials I Have on Hand	Materials Needed	Priority in Purchasing
	Dramatic play	Dramatic play	Top priority items (essential for licensure)
	Music and movement	Music and movement	
	Manipulatives	Manipulatives	Items needed soon (within six months)
	Arts and crafts	Arts and crafts	
	Books	Books	
	Outdoor playthings	Outdoor playthings	Wish list items
	Furniture	Furniture	

Appendix F:
Outdoor Home Playground Safety Checklist

Use this to help make your home playground a safe place to play.

Supervision	Be sure to always supervise children on play equipment.
Surfacing	Install a protective surface under and around play equipment to reduce the likelihood of serious head injuries. • For most play equipment, install protective surfacing six feet in all directions beyond the equipment. • For swings, extend the protective surfacing in front and in back of the swing to a distance that is twice the height of the bar from which the swing is suspended. • For tire swings, install protective surfacing outward from the swing equal to the suspension chain plus six feet.
Types of surfacing	Carpeting and thin mats are not adequate as protective surfacing. Maintain at least nine inches of loose-fill material or use an ASTM F1292–rated material at the depth required for the equipment height. • Use wood mulch or chips, shredded rubber mulch, or engineered wood fiber for equipment up to eight feet high. • Use sand, pea gravel, or mulch products listed above for play equipment up to five feet high. • Use surface mats tested to provide impact protection equal to or greater than the height of the play equipment.
Equipment maintenance	Periodically check nuts, bolts, caps, swing seats, suspension ropes, chains, and cables, and replace them as necessary. Maintain loose-fill surfacing and surface mats.
Opening	Eliminate openings that can trap a child's head or neck, such as openings in guardrails or ladders. Openings should be smaller than three and a half inches to prevent entry of a small child's body or larger than nine inches to allow a child's head and body to slide completely through.
Ropes	Never attach jump ropes, clotheslines, pet leashes, or cords of any kind to play equipment. Anchor any climbing ropes at both ends. Remove drawstrings from children's clothes. Children can strangle on these.
Anchors	Bury or cover anchors with adequate surfacing material to prevent tripping. Play equipment should not tip over.
Guardrails or barriers	Make sure that platforms and ramps over thirty inches high have guardrails or barriers to prevent falls.
Repair	Repair sharp points or edges on equipment that can cause injuries.
Upkeep of hardware	Replace missing hardware, eliminate protruding bolts, and close "S" hooks that can cause injuries.

From the *Outdoor Home Playground Safety Handbook* by the U.S. Consumer Product Safety Commission (CPSC), published 2005. The complete public-domain handbook is available for download at www.cpsc.gov/cpscpub/pubs/324.pdf.

Appendix G: Website Resources

American Council on Science and Health (ACSH)
www.acsh.org
The ACSH is a nonprofit association that seeks to educate consumers on topics related to health, environment, and lifestyle choices. This website offers resources and publications related to current public policies.

BabyCenter
www.babycenter.com
This resource provides information related to many stages of motherhood, from trying to conceive to childhood. Expert advice, forums for discussion between users, and various articles can be accessed here.

Center for Inclusive Design and Environmental Access
www.udeworld.com
www.ap.buffalo.edu/idea
The IDeA seeks to promote universal design, in which buildings are easily accessible to people with and without physical disabilities. These resources emphasize the importance of simplicity and accessibility in architecture.

Consumer Product Safety Commission
www.cpsc.gov
www.recalls.gov
These U.S. government sites provide information related to product recalls and allow users to report injuries associated with products.

Department of Justice
www.ada.gov/childq&a.htm
This U.S. government site provides information and technical assistance on the Americans with Disabilities Act.

Environmental Protection Agency
www.epa.gov
This U.S. government site provides information on topics related to the natural environment and its relation to health as well as a quick reference to environmental laws and regulations.

Environments, Inc.
www.eichild.com
This organization designs, manufactures, and distributes furniture, educational equipment, and toys for young children. The website also offers curriculum materials and other resources for creating environments for young children.

Go Green Rating Scale
www.gogreenratingscale.org
This website offers support for users and potential users of the *Go Green Rating Scale for Early Childhood Settings*, published by Redleaf Press.

Health House
www.healthhouse.org
Created in conjunction with the American Lung Association, this website provides access to resources related to building and maintaining houses with health in mind.

HolisticOnline (Health and Wellness)
www.holisticonline.com
This website provides information related to alternative medical practices, holistic living, and nutrition, and acts as a database for a multitude of outside links pertaining to holistic living.

Housecleaning Tips
www.housecleaning-tips.com
This website supplies users with a plan for more efficient housecleaning. Additionally, it offers tips for cleaning individual sections of a home.

Institute for Challenging Disorganization (ICD)
www.challengingdisorganization.org
The ICD provides assistance and referrals for people affected by chronic disorganization. This resource provides information, organizing techniques, and solutions to professional organizers, related professionals, and the public.

National Association for the Education of Young Children (NAEYC)
www.naeyc.org
The NAEYC focuses on advances in children's educational and developmental services. This website offers information about membership, accreditation, conferences, and links to related websites.

National Association for Family Child Care (NAFCC)
http://nafcc.net
The NAFCC provides programs related to child care training and seeks to strengthen the reputation of child care services nationally. This resource provides information pertaining to conference dates, accreditation processes, and memberships.

National Association of Child Care Resource and Referral Agencies (NACCRRA)
www.naccrra.org
The NACCRRA provides programs and services to child care providers across the country. This website provides plentiful information such as articles and research for families and child care providers.

National Resource Center for Health and Safety in Child Care and Early Education (NRC)
www.nrckids.org
The NRC seeks to educate families, child care professionals, and regulators on the importance of health and safety in child care centers. This website offers user toolkits and guides for enhancing centers, and provides steps necessary to create a healthy, safe environment for children.

National Safety Council
www.nsc.org
This organization seeks to reduce workplace injury and death, and further promotes safety at home and on the road. The website offers statistics, publications, and resources.

Toy Industry Association, Inc.
www.toy-tia.org
This website serves as a forum for members of the Toy Industry Association to access new legislation, bulletins, and other subjects. Also, to promote their goals of safety and growth in the toy industry, the site provides information about toy safety.

References

BC Family Child Care Association. 2005. *Creating a Child Care Environment for Success*. Surry, BC: BC Family Child Care Association. www.bcfcca.ca /participant_resources.php.

Boise, Phil. 2010. *Go Green Rating Scale for Early Childhood Settings*. St. Paul, MN: Redleaf Press.

Consumer Product Safety Commission (CPSC). 2005. *Handbook for Playground Safety*. CPSC publication number 325. www.cpsc.gov.

———. 2010. "Safety Standards for Full-Size Baby Cribs and Non-Full-Size Baby Cribs: Final Rule." *Federal Register* 75 (248): 81766–88.

Curtis, Deb, and Margie Carter. 2003. *Designs for Living and Learning: Transforming Early Childhood Environments*. St. Paul, MN: Redleaf Press.

Daggett, Willard R., Jeffrey E. Cobble, and Steven J. Gertel. 2008. "Color in an Optimum Learning Environment." International Center for Leadership in Education. www.leadered.com/pdf/color%20white%20paper.pdf.

Davis, Kim. 2005. *Creating Outdoor Environments for Learning and Fun*. Early Childhood Module Series. Bloomington: Indiana University–Bloomington.

Erba, Giuseppe. 2006. "Shedding Light on Photosensitivity, One of Epilepsy's Most Complex Conditions." Posted March 6. Epilepsy Foundation. www.epilepsyfoun dation.org/about/photosensitivity/gerba.cfm.

Ferguson, Barbara. 1986. *How to Design & Build Children's Play Equipment*. San Ramon, CA: Ortho Books.

Giacopini, Elena. 1997. "Infant-Toddler Schools of Reggio Emilia: Comune di Reggio Emilia, Italy." Paper presented at the Reggio Emilia Winter Institute, Reggio Emilia, Italy.

Gilberg, Lynne, ed. 2000. *Ideas for Great Kids' Rooms*. Birmingham, AL: Oxmoor House, Inc.

Goldstein, Kurt, and Martin Scheerer. 1941. "Abstract and Concrete Behavior: An Experimental Study with Special Tests." *Psychological Monographs* 53 (2): 1–151.

Greenman, Jim. 2005. *Caring Spaces, Learning Places: Children's Environments That Work*. Redmond, WA: Exchange Press, Inc.

———. 2006. "The Importance of Order." *Exchange Magazine* 170 (July/August): 53–55.

Harms, Thelma, Debby Cryer, and Richard Clifford. 2007. *Family Child Care Environment Rating Scale*, rev. ed. New York: Teachers College Press.

Hathaway, Warren E., John A. Hargreaves, Gordon W. Thompson, and Dennis Novitsky. 1992. "A Study into the Effects of Light on Children of Elementary

School Age: A Case of Daylight Robbery." Alberta, Canada: Alberta Policy and Planning Branch, Alberta Education Planning and Information Services Division.

Isbell, Rebecca, and Betty Exelby. 2001. *Early Learning Environments That Work*. Beltsville, MD: Gryphon House, Inc.

Isenberg, Joan Packer, and Nancy Quisenberry. 2002. "Play: Essential for All Children. A Position Paper of the Association for Childhood Education International." *Childhood Education* 79 (1): 33–39. www.udel.edu/bateman/acei /playpaper.htm.

Kamrin, Michael. 2001. *The Scientific Facts about the Dry-Cleaning Chemical Perc*. New York: American Council on Science and Health. www.acsh.org.

Kelly, David J., Shaoying Liu, Liezhong Ge, Paul C. Quinn, Alan M. Slater, Kang Lee, Qinyao Liu, and Oliver Pascalis. 2007. "Cross-Race Preferences for Same-Race Faces Extend beyond the African versus Caucasian Contrast in 3-Month-Old Infants." *Infancy* 11 (1): 87–95.

Layzer, Jean I., Barbara D. Goodson, and Melanie Brown-Lyons. 2007. *Care in the Home: A Description of Family Child Care and the Experiences of the Families and Children Who Use It*. Final report. Cambridge, MA: U.S. Department of Health and Human Services Administration for Children and Families.

Mayo Clinic. 2009. "Seasonal Affective Disorder (SAD): Treatments and Drugs." Posted September 24. http://www.mayoclinic.com/health/ seasonal-affective-disorder/DS00195/DSECTION=prevention.

Mehrabian, Albert. 1976. *Public Places and Private Spaces: The Psychology of Work, Play, and Living Environments*. New York: Basic Books, Inc.

Morrissey, Taryn, and Patti Banghart. 2007. *Family Child Care in the United States*. New York: Child Care and Early Education Research Connection.

National Association for Family Child Care. 2005. *Quality Standards for NAFCC Accreditation*, 4th ed. Salt Lake City: National Association for Family Child Care.

National Association of Child Care Resources and Referral Agencies. 2010. *Child Care in America: 2010 State Fact Sheets*. Arlington, VA: National Association of Child Care Resources and Referral Agencies.

Olds, Anita Rui. 1997. "Mood: The Spirit of Place." *Beginnings Workshop: Room Arrangement Exchange* (September).

———. 2001. *Child Care Design Guide*. New York: McGraw-Hill.

Painter, Marylyn. 1976. "Fluorescent Lights and Hyperactivity in Children: An Experiment." *Academic Therapy* 12 (2): 181–84.

Prescott, Elizabeth. 1994. "The Physical Environment—A Powerful Regulator of Experience." *Child Care Information Exchange* 100: 34–37.

Saul, Jane D., and Betsy Saul. 2001. "Multicultural Activities throughout the Year." *Multicultural Education* 8 (4): 38–40.

Schreiber, Mary Ellis. 1996. "Lighting Alternatives: Considerations for Child Care Centers." *Young Children* 51 (4): 11–13.

Shepherd, Wendy, and Jennifer Eaton. 1997. "Creating Environments that Intrigue and Delight Children and Adults." *Child Care Information Exchange* 117:42–47.

Steele, Jennifer, Y. Susan Choi, and Nalini Ambady. 2004. "Stereotyping, Prejudice, and Discrimination: The Effect of Group Based Expectations on Moral Functioning." In *Nurturing Morality*, edited by Theresa A. Thorkildsen and Herbert J. Walberg, 77–98. New York: Kluwer Academic.

Tanner, Kenneth. 2000. *Essential Aspects of Designing a School*. Athens: University of Georgia.

U.S. Congress. 2008. *Consumer Product Safety Improvement Act of 2008*. Public Law 110-314. *U.S. Statutes at Large* 112:3016–77.

U.S. Environmental Protection Agency. 2003. *Protect Your Family from Lead in Your Home*. Washington, DC: U.S. Environmental Protection Agency.

———. 2008. *Children's Environmental Health: 2008 Highlights*. Washington, DC: U.S. Environmental Protection Agency.

———. 2010. "Asbestos in Your Home." Updated June 7. http://www.epa.gov /asbestos/pubs/ashome.html.

Vicars, Dennis. 2010. "The Beauty of the Acronym! Good Management Begins with Good People." *Exchange Magazine* 193:18–19.